PROPHETIC RAGE

PROPHETIC CHRISTIANITY

Series Editors

Bruce Ellis Benson
Malinda Elizabeth Berry
Peter Goodwin Heltzel

The Prophetic Christianity series explores the complex relationship between Christian doctrine and contemporary life. Deeply rooted in the Christian tradition yet taking postmodern and postcolonial perspectives seriously, series authors navigate difference and dialogue constructively about divisive and urgent issues of the early twenty-first century. The books in the series are sensitive to historical contexts, marked by philosophical precision, and relevant to contemporary problems. Embracing shalom justice, series authors seek to bear witness to God's gracious activity of building beloved community.

PUBLISHED

Bruce Ellis Benson, Malinda Elizabeth Berry, and Peter Goodwin Heltzel, eds., *Prophetic Evangelicals: Envisioning a Just and Peaceable Kingdom* (2012)

Peter Goodwin Heltzel, *Resurrection City: A Theology of Improvisation* (2012)

Johnny Bernard Hill, *Prophetic Rage: A Postcolonial Theology of Liberation* (2013)

Randy S. Woodley, *Shalom and the Community of Creation: An Indigenous Vision* (2012)

Prophetic Rage

A Postcolonial Theology
of Liberation

Johnny Bernard Hill

WILLIAM B. EERDMANS PUBLISHING COMPANY
GRAND RAPIDS, MICHIGAN / CAMBRIDGE, U.K.

Published 2013 by
Wm. B. Eerdmans Publishing Co.
2140 Oak Industrial Drive N.E., Grand Rapids, Michigan 49505 /
P.O. Box 163, Cambridge CB3 9PU U.K.

Library of Congress Cataloging-in-Publication Data

Hill, Johnny Bernard.
Prophetic rage: a postcolonial theology of liberation / Johnny Bernard Hill.
pages   cm. — (Prophetic Christianity)
Includes bibliographical references and index.
ISBN 978-0-8028-6977-7 (pbk.: alk. paper)
1. Liberation theology. 2. Postcolonial theology.   I. Title.

BT83.57.H55   2013

230′.0464 — dc23

2013022266

www.eerdmans.com

For the Voiceless

Contents

Acknowledgments

We can do absolutely nothing without the support of community. Those persons who have surrounded me (colleagues, friends, family, and students) have been and continue to be the wind in my sails. Without them, nothing would be possible. First and foremost, the editors of this series (Bruce Ellis Benson, Malinda Elizabeth Berry, and Peter Goodwin Heltzel) are to be celebrated and applauded for introducing such a series at this important moment in history. Their prophetic imagination and keen intellectual precision have made possible this present work; to them I am forever thankful. I would like to offer a special debt of gratitude to Paul Myhre and the Wabash Center for Religion and Theology for the very generous gift of the Research Fellowship, and to the staff of the Association of Theological Schools, Steven Graham and Dan Aleshire, for the support of the Theological Scholars Grant. Both grants helped to support the research of the project, and for that I am eternally grateful. The title for this book was inspired by a presentation delivered by Mark Taylor at the American Academy of Religion in 2008. I am very appreciative of his courageous and creative witness for justice and liberation.

This book is the product of many lectures, presentations, sermons, and exchanges that have taken place in recent years. I would like to thank students, friends, and colleagues at those communities, such as the University of Chicago, Garrett-Evangelical Theological Seminary, Johns Hopkins University, Bellarmine University, McAfee School of Theology at Mercer University, Pittsburgh Theological Seminary, Spalding University,

Acknowledgments

Shiloh Baptist Church of Plainfield, New Jersey, and Morning Star Baptist Church of Queens, New York.

I would like to offer a special word of thanks and appreciation to the students, friends, and colleagues at the Interdenominational Theological Center in Atlanta, Georgia. Thank you for reminding me of the power of Sankofa and the ways in which Christianity at its best is prophetic. Colleagues such as Dr. C. T. Vivian, Stephen Ray, Karen Jackson-Weaver, Young Lee Hertig, Walter Silva Thompson, Gerald Lamont Thomas, Amy Plantinga Pauw, Ken Walden, Robin Dease, Monica Coleman, Peter Heltzel, Ronald Peters, and many others were incredibly helpful in their words of wisdom as well. I thank my students at Louisville Seminary, the Interdenominational Theological Center, and Claflin University for challenging me with their questions and reflections, and in particular, Adam Clark and Darvin Adams for assisting with the research for the book.

My children, Regan and Jonathan, are so wonderful and truly make life worth living. They are my inspiration, and to them I say thank you for their sacrifice and support of this work.

Introduction

"I hate, I despise your religious feasts;
   I cannot stand your assemblies.
Even though you bring me burnt offerings and grain offerings,
   I will not accept them.
Though you bring choice fellowship offerings,
   I will have no regard for them.
Away with the noise of your songs!
   I will not listen to the music of your harps.
But let justice roll on like a river,
   righteousness like a never-failing stream!"

(Amos 5:21-24 NIV)

Revolution is mankind's way of life today. This is the age of revolution; the "age of indifference" is gone forever. But the latter age paved the way for today; for the great masses of mankind, while still suffering the greatest oppression and the greatest affronts to their dignity as human beings, never ceased to resist, to fight as well as they could, to live in combat. The combatant dignity of humanity was maintained in an unbreakable though not always visible line, in the depths of the life of the masses and in the uninterrupted fight — slandered, attacked, but alive in the very center of history — of little revolutionary vanguards bound to this profound human reality and to its socialist future, and not to the ap-

1

parent omnipotence of great systems. . . . Today the great systems have died or are living in a state of crisis. And it is no longer the age of little vanguards. The whole of humanity has erupted violently, tumultuously onto the stage of history, taking its own destiny in its hands.[1]

Prophetic Rage is a manifesto of liberation, hope, and reconciliation. It is the cry of millions from around the world, both Christian and non-Christian, representing all races and ethnicities, genders, sexual orientations, and faiths, yearning to be free, to be whole, to flourish. Inspired by the long and creative legacy of prophetic Christianity, *Prophetic Rage* is the call for renewal and transformation in the quest to resist empire and establish alternative spheres of peace, justice, reconciliation, hope, and redemption in the world. It represents the challenge of establishing a political theology of difference, rooted in the prophetic call for justice and reconciliation in the church and society. By summoning and reclaiming the prophetic dimensions of black religion and black theology's challenge to white supremacy, *Prophetic Rage* offers a new vision for resisting and overcoming empire, and its related tentacles of racism, patriarchy, violence and militarism, and economic exploitation. Beverly W. Harrison observes in "The Power of Anger in the Work of Love: Christian Ethics for Women and Other Strangers" that women's bodies have taught us great lessons about the power of righteous anger, so prophetic rage is insightful as we think about forging a constructive postcolonial theology of liberation for our present age.[2]

Prophetic rage courses through my veins. I am the great-great-grandson of the enslaved. I was raised in the gutbucket belly of the South, grandson of a sharecropper. My mother cleared bedpans and tended to the wounds of the sick and dying bodies of white racists. My father was a sanitation worker, not unlike those that Martin Luther King Jr. marched for and subsequently died for in Memphis, Tennessee, on April 4, 1968. In a real sense, Dr. King gave his life standing and fighting for my father, a hardworking, decent man, tall and strong. The rage that beats in my heart is a righ-

1. Frantz Fanon, *A Dying Colonialism*, trans. Haakon Chevalier, introduction by Adolfo Gilly (New York: Grove Press, 1965), 1.

2. Beverly W. Harrison, "The Power of Anger in the Work of Love: Christian Ethics for Women and Other Strangers," *Union Quarterly Review* 36 (1981): 41-57, reprinted in Harrison's *Making the Connections: Essays in Feminist Social Ethics* (Minnetonka, Minn.: Olympic Marketing Corp., 1985), 3-21.

teous rage, grounded in the love for humanity, yet yearning for redemption and hope. Because of what Dr. King represents, and sacrificed for men like my father, the sanitation worker, I have dedicated my life, heart, and soul to fight, resist, and struggle for the cause of freedom, justice, and equality. It is through this lens that I make the case that prophetic rage is a necessary prescriptive response to the present culture of imperialism and nihilism.

We now stand in a time of remembrance. The great revolutionary movements of yesterday have given way to the stigmatizing forces of consumerism, materialism, and violence. It is time to reflect on the state of humanity. Now is the time to sound the trumpet of justice and human dignity once again, as did the great modernist thinkers of the Enlightenment period. On the 150th anniversary of the signing of the Emancipation Proclamation in 1863, and the 50th anniversary of the historic March on Washington in 1963, the urgency of forging a new theological vision that is inclusive, multidimensional, yet grounded in the particularity of a people's contextual experience, has become blatantly clear, as struggles for justice and human dignity have become so insidiously entrenched in mainstream society.

Prophetic Rage and the Quest for Human Dignity

One aspect of the enduring legacy of slavery, colonialism, and racism in the modern era is found in the assertion that somehow black life is solely of concern to black peoples, that black life has very little to teach the rest of the world. However, we are discovering now more than ever before that the last very well may be first and the first very well may be last. The decline of Western culture, along with the crippling reality of secularization and nihilism, means we must look elsewhere for hope and possibility. And since the destiny of the world and its inhabitants is intertwined with the fate of the Western world, we are now faced with mutual hope and transformation or the reality of mutual destruction and damnation. I agree with Leonardo Boff, who proclaimed the emergence of a new global civilization, a new global society, being brought into being largely by the rise of technology, mass communication, and transcontinental travel. This global age means rethinking the meaning of human dignity and personhood in a day when the voices of the oppressed are being suppressed behind the guise of technological and consumeristic progress. The illusion of so-called progress could not be more contradictory than in the lives of black bodies in cities across the United States, in the diaspora, and in the developing world. The destiny and fate of humanity may well be inextricably bound up in the plight of humanity's darker peoples.

By reflecting on the ways in which black life has resisted and challenged the onslaught of suffering and meaninglessness that has arrived in the demons of slavery, colonialism, genocide, Jim Crow segregation, and apartheid, we may well have much to say about how to attend to the great struggles of empire and nihilism today. The central motif of *Prophetic Rage* expands the gaze of black theology and black religion in a way that gives voice to the multiplicity of human suffering in the global world. The forces of globalization and technology, and the totalizing effects of empire, have exposed the ways in which struggles of freedom and human dignity are indivisible. *Prophetic Rage* shows how the black experience, in its resistance to nihilism and empire, may point the way forward as individuals and groups in America and around the world struggle to overcome the legacy of slavery, colonialism, and patriarchal systems, both individually and collectively.

Liberation is multidimensional, and so is human experience. The rigid compartmentalization and boxes that restricted dialogue and fluidity of ideas are fading away. Moving and flowing within human bodies are complex, multilayered, and dynamic identities. This means that, inasmuch as liberation may appear in different forms, what binds them together is a common demand for freedom and justice, to be heard and to seek human fulfillment. *Prophetic Rage* recognizes the multiplicity of oppressive systems and the gift of black people's lives in offering a way forward for the human family in overcoming the stagnating and destructive forces of nihilism and empire.

Theologies of liberation and resistance — feminist theologies, black theologies of liberation, Latin American liberation theology, as well as *mujerista* theologies, *minjung* theologies, gay and lesbian theologies and queer theologies — all share a common demand for the voice of the voiceless to be heard. What distinguishes these theologies is their contextual emphasis, the belief that social location is what orients and grounds theology. They stand in sharp contrast to the colonizing, grand narratives that marked the modern world. *Prophetic Rage* reflects the ways in which black religion has typified the struggle for oppressed and marginalized voices in the context of their particular experience to resist empire, and fight for freedom, justice, and human dignity.

I have seen this at work in my own experience. I was raised as a black boy in the Deep South, on a dirt road on the edge of an old plantation. As Langston Hughes said, "I've known rivers: I have known rivers ancient as the world and older than the flow of human blood in human veins." In the

South, we were poor but loved. We experienced hardship but lived with dignity. I shared a small country house with seven sisters, each full of grace and love and dignity. They were young but strong and wise. They carried with them the blood of slave women like Sojourner Truth, Harriet Tubman, and Harriet Jacobs. Like me, they toiled in tobacco fields as children to help feed the family and to purchase school clothes. They were mocked and ridiculed by their peers, but they never acquiesced to the dehumanizing structures of patriarchy, racism, and white supremacy that were and continue to be normative in the South. In my black male body, I carry the memory, experience, and wisdom of my sisters and their plight. As with my father whose hands carried the sewage and scum of society and my mother who dressed the wounds of dying humanity, I lift up the voices of my seven sisters, voices discarded by the noise of empire and the threat of nihilism itself.

Prophetic Rage and Resistance to Empire

I was born after the civil rights struggle. The memory of Martin Luther King Jr.'s great speeches, the militancy of black power, and the poetically passionate pleas of activists and revolutionaries had all but dissipated. As a child born in the 1970s, what I inherited was the crushing consequences of globalization and postindustrialism. The great factory jobs across the nation, especially in the South, were transported overseas. Well-paying jobs that stabilized communities and offered a sense of dignity and livelihood for families could no longer be looked upon with any sense of assurance. All that was left were abandoned communities, unemployment, homelessness, failing school systems, and the meandering escapism of drug addiction, crack cocaine, violence, and suffering. Now, it would seem, at every street corner, shopping mall, online store, website, bookstore, city park, coffeehouse, restaurant, or latrine, the sting of hurt, pain, and despair nags at blacks and others like flies on a sore under the weight of Georgia heat on a summer afternoon. The globalization and commercialization of hip-hop and popular culture, a hallmark achievement of the reality of secularization and cultural nihilism, have rendered black theology at best suspect, at worst emphatically irrelevant to the task of liberation.

Since James Cone's release of *Black Theology and Black Power* in 1969, and even since his recent book, *The Cross and the Lynching Tree*, black theologians in particular have tried to articulate the suffering of black people in America and liberation from white racism in America. Today, there is a need to reintroduce black theology to a new generation of thinkers, and also to recontextualize the black theological task in light of the reconfiguration of global society. This need also arises out of the postmodern dilemma, the problem of nihilism, as well as the social, political, and economic context ushered in by a new age of technology, globalization, and empire.

The most powerful way to resist meaninglessness is prophetic rage, or the refusal to accept the realities of structural injustice such as poverty, escalating militarism, genocide, and housing discrimination. I suggest that black theology may also provide a gateway or insights into the prospects of overcoming the broader quest for meaning in Western society in particular. I believe I am not alone when I say that the present conditions before blacks throughout the African diaspora require the kind of courageous faith, dangerous discipleship, and unapologetic prophetic rage that circulated through the veins of those ancient prophets like Moses, Amos, Isaiah, Micah, Habakkuk, and Jeremiah, and lived in the zealous pilgrimages of souls like Sojourner Truth, Fannie Lou Hamer, Mary McLeod Bethune, Malcolm X, Martin Luther King Jr., and even present-day truth-tellers like Nas, Common, Missy Elliott, Alicia Keys, and Kanye West. In the same manner that black South Africans were compelled to question the very legitimacy of the apartheid government, black folks of every hue are also driven to ask, does the land that black folks have bled for, fought for, died for, and cried for, since the inception of this modern experiment, have the kind of democracy that is of black people, for black people, and by black people? In a time when the nation is at war, not only with a foreign enemy but also with itself over its own ideals, history, and destiny, black folks must begin to ponder once again what it means to be human and Christian in today's post-Katrina, Jena Six, poverty-stricken America. On a larger scale, if America, as the lone superpower of the modern world that has now produced perhaps the greatest militaristic monster in human history, has its fate inextricably bound to the rest of the world through an ever increasingly globalized economy, it may very well be that the promise of human survival and flourishing on the planet rests with the prophetic witness of black folks, and others who share their plight, in this mammoth imperial beast of the new world order.

Understanding the nature of empire and its relationship to the black experience creates the space to understand the ways in which blacks share a common struggle of resistance alongside other oppressed bodies in the modern and postcolonial world. By recognizing that the black experience, from slavery and colonialism to Jim Crow segregation and mass incarceration, exposes empire for its violence and all-consuming nature, the door opens to resist and dismantle related systems of marginality and injustice as well. I agree with Nestor Miguez, Joerg Rieger, and Jung Mo Sung, who, in *Beyond the Spirit of Empire*, described empire as a "way of exercising power through different legalities (and illegalities)."[3] The World Alliance of Reformed Churches (WARC) described empire as "the convergence of economic, political, cultural and military interests that constitute a system of domination in which benefits flow primarily to the powerful. Centred in the last remaining superpower, yet spread all over the world, empire crosses all boundaries, reconstructs identities, subverts cultures, overcomes nation states and challenges religious communities."[4]

While the language of empire is receiving renewed attention today, the black experience with empire, up through the events of transcontinental slavery, struggles with apartheid and Jim Crow segregation, and lynching, has revealed not simply the horrors and perversity of empire; it has also unveiled the creative power of black protest and hope (infused with Christian love, forgiveness, and reconciliation) as a means of resisting and overcoming its destructive darts of nihilism and domination. Blacks' prophetic refusal to surrender and their desire to maintain hope amid dark clouds of despair reveal the weaknesses and vulnerabilities of empire. Even when discarded, black bodies emerged with a fierce and determined hope, a forceful struggle to be human and exist as free moral agents.

Today, black life, whether in prisons, nursing homes, crumbling ghettos, roach-infested trailers, or urine-consumed alleyways, must no longer be discarded into the wasteland of indifference and shame. Too many people are suffering for those of us who claim to follow the God of the prophets, the children of Israel, Jesus, and the martyred saints of history to find refuge behind false notions of achievement, fame, capitalistic desire, intellectual isolation, and a shallow pop culture of consumption and stifling individual gratification. The only appropriate, and possibly reasonable, response is prophetic rage — not the kind of rage that leads to bitterness, hatred, violence, hopelessness, and despair, but the kind of indignation that insists on processes of prophetic action, transformation, truth telling, and courageous risk taking for the present moment.

3. Nestor Miguez, Joerg Rieger, and Jung Mo Sung, *Beyond the Spirit of Empire: Theology and Politics in a New Key* (London: SCM, 2009), 3.

4. Miguez, Rieger, and Sung, *Beyond the Spirit*, 5. See the report from the 24th General Council of the WARC, in Accra, Ghana, in 2004, entitled "Globalization and Empire: A Challenge to Christian Mission."

I approach the task of addressing these questions not as a detached, unbiased academic, but as a survivor, victim, parent, brother, friend, priest, preacher, and child of humanity who, like many of my generation, is fed up with (no, downright sick of) faith, theology, the church, scholarship, and even esoteric conceptions of God that have nothing meaningful to say to the reality of human suffering in the world. So-called postmodern scholars wish to say that humanity has now reached a point in which it will either self-destruct by its own thirst for power, greed, and selfishness or burst open into a new, more complex interrelated world of fluid consciousness and sharing, a world that recognizes itself as that which Leonardo Boff describes as "an enormous living organism." What has not been addressed are the ways in which ordinary narratives of the black experience and cultural life in general are indispensable resources for challenging the nihilistic threat.

Why Prophetic Rage? Why Now?

History has proven that whenever a civilization or culture has had to confront the chilling sting of nihilism, those who survived emerged with prophetic zeal to resist and speak with a resounding voice to the silence of despair. Poor blacks throughout the African diaspora, and certainly the world's poor in general, are, like the psalmist, singing,

> By the rivers of Babylon —
>> there we sat down and there we wept
>> when we remembered Zion. (Ps. 137:1 NRSV)

New realities of globalization and technology, creating cultures of abundance for the few and cultures of scarcity and survival for the many, now demand a theological response rooted in radical praxis, echoing the voices of the ancient biblical prophets and those of the church. With the recent rise of President Barack Obama, it is clear that a new paradigmatic moment is sweeping across the American geopolitical landscape and perhaps the world. Through the shackles of nihilism, a persistent cry of hope and revolutionary change is swelling up from the depths of ordinary human experiences.

Under the weight of empire and its systemic companion, globalization (as an economic ideology and exploitative reality of a free market economy), the masses of poor people worldwide are yearning for creative responses from both the church and society. The statistical data reflecting the disparities of blacks today are compelling. For instance, according to a report from Human Rights Watch, 910,000 of the 2,100,000 inmates in America's prisons are African American.[5] The church must begin to raise critical systematic questions along with former U.S. Surgeon General David Satcher, when he states that "African American and Latino children make up more than 80 percent of pediatric AIDS cases."[6] Those living in prison cells, slums, and ghettos from Chicago to Nairobi; sufferers in HIV/AIDS hospice wards; teary-eyed mothers of gang violence victims; and the lonely nomadic homeless souls throughout America and the world, in their lingering deprivation, are calling for the kind of faith that means something. They are questioning in passionate ways the inadequacy of Christianity as a historical and institutional system. Christianity must be as much about *being* as it is about believing in the present age. As the mystical theologian Howard Thurman wrote more than half a century ago in his autobiography, *With Head and Heart,* the Christian church (and perhaps Western culture more broadly speaking) must integrate the intellectual toughness of rationalism with the prophetic courage of a compassionate heart.

Nearly a generation after the assassination of Martin Luther King Jr. on April 4, 1968, on the balcony of the Lorraine Hotel in Memphis, a desperate cry of hope has rippled across the black experience (and more broadly the world's poor) as to the promise of meaningful change. If the Italian philosopher Gianni Vattimo is correct in his prediction that the greatest threat to postmodern society is nihilism, the current mood in many poor black communities is perhaps the ultimate test. According to William Julius Wilson, a frightening economic stagnation is emerging among the urban black poor, as well as in rural spaces, set off by the radical global economic reconfigurations that took flight in the early 1970s. As many American companies jumped ship in search of increased profits, industrialization moved overseas, while an ill-equipped and bewildered urban labor class was abandoned and left unprepared to meet the challenges of a rising technocratic culture.

James Cone, Major Jones, Cecil Cone, Gayraud Wilmore, Katie Cannon, J. Deotis Roberts, and other pioneers of the black theology and womanist movements provided a courageous theological landscape pri-

---

5. "Incarcerated America," Figure 1, at http://www.hrw.org/backgrounder/usa/incarceration/uso42903.pdf, April 2003, Human Rights Watch; also in *The Covenant with Black America* (Chicago: Third World Press, 2006), 53.

6. Centers for Disease Control and Prevention, HIV/AIDS Fact Sheet, at http://www.cdc.gov/omh/AMH/factsheets/hiv.htm#1.

marily shaped by the civil rights movement. The sharpest differences within black theology, black religion, and black political thought emerged from Cone and Roberts. Both figures were highly regarded theologians in their fields and deeply concerned about the nature of the church's witness to social issues. These resources are considerable and beyond measure. At the same time, if the civil rights movement is to continue to have meaning and merit for critical study for scholars and students, it must speak with urgent relevancy to the pain and suffering of black people today. There is a dangerously deceptive quality of the struggle for justice in today's post-Katrina, post-9/11 world where human suffering is hidden behind the veil of capitalistic desire, consumption, infotainment culture, and technological advances. One of the major assumptions functioning in political thought arising out of the civil rights movement was a presumption of moral goodness, consciousness, and positive progressivism. Many truly believed that if only the oppressed could lay hold of that radical vision of community and the eschatological hope spoken of in the eloquent words of the young black preacher from Georgia, then a brighter day would come. And indeed it did. For countless numbers of blacks, the civil rights movement opened the door to an instant arena of opportunity and financial gain. What the posthumous whirlwind of an ending Vietnam/Nixon era did not account for was a ferocious white backlash and the reordering of a sophisticated conservative agenda that continues to wreak havoc today.

Ultimately, I am interested in advancing a constructive political, theological, and social analysis that considers critical contemporary questions including contemporary political thought, technology, hip-hop, liberation theologies, and economics. I am not interested in rehashing the verbiage of classical theological dogmatism that does not speak to the suffering of oppressed people. When I speak of oppressed peoples, I speak of those empty-bellied souls living on the edge of life and death, on the verge of suicide, on the margins of our communities. I speak of those who live in long soup kitchen lines, who struggle to feed their children; daily sustenance or "hand-to-mouth" living is their chief priority. I speak of those Frantz Fanon called the "wretched of the earth." When considering present-day questions about black identity, it would seem that Fanon (in dialogue with Michel Foucault, Gilles Deleuze, Cornel West, and John Stuart Hall, other critics of modernity) still has a great deal to say to us today who wish to understand the crippling fragmentation and abnegation felt by many poor African American communities in particular.

There seems to be an agitating antagonism toward the black poor today, both within and beyond the black community. Culturally, the language of oppression has now turned inward, inasmuch as there is an unchecked cultural assumption that somehow the poor are responsible for their own poverty. What I find most interesting is that this assumption is rarely challenged by the religious establishment. As Marian Wright Edelman recognized, the fact that millions of children live in poverty in a culture that celebrates uncontrollable profligate consumption is indeed an amazing moral contradiction, particularly in a nation that claims to be overwhelmingly Christian. So any message of liberation in today's context must be unapologetically addressed to oppressed people. This is indeed a difficult and dangerous task. Although they don't often say it, many despise the poor. In an age Nicholas Wolterstorff describes as "victorious living," Christians especially must reclaim that radical vision of community and solidarity with the poor, as did that first-century Nazarene two thousand years ago. This task is challenging because, for the most part, blacks do not control the channels of communication. Almost all the modes of communication in America are controlled by a few media moguls. Perhaps with the exception of cyberspace, much of what is seen and heard comes from persons who often show little regard for the suffering of the downtrodden.

In many ways, the language of postmodern discourse has been hijacked by the right-wing assertion that Christian theology has no business mingling in the worldly activities of political pandering. After all, if there is one thing postmodern thought teaches us, it is that there is an insatiable "incredulity of metanarratives."[7] In other words, any so-called radical totalizing vision injected into the scrutiny of public discourse is destined to crumble under the pressure of skepticism and rejection. Since John Milbank's book *Theology and Social Theory,* and to a lesser extent Alasdair MacIntyre's incomparable *After Virtue,* many scholars (particularly neoliberals) have interpreted postmodern thought to offer a way of challenging and even undermining the legitimacy of liberation theologies.

As Christians, particularly in the West, stand at the so-called "end of history," the loud and ambitious cries of the voiceless refuse to drift out into the restless seas of nihilism and indifference. It seems that in spite of repeated efforts to suppress the liberationist call for resistance and transformation, there is an unshakable desire to recognize a form of Christianity not necessarily grounded in the creeds, doctrines, and impassive theol-

7. Jean-François Lyotard, *The Postmodern Condition: A Report on Knowledge,* trans. Geoff Bennington and Brian Massumi (Minneapolis: University of Minnesota Press, 1984).

ogies of old, but in a God who cares deeply and profoundly for those who suffer and makes that caring and concern known in concrete ways. One could easily conclude by the lack of intense debate in many sectors of the church, the academy, and society at large that somehow suffering no longer exists. After all, new names are being added to the coveted *Forbes* list of billionaires each week. Judging from mainstream media, it is hard to image that there is any problem at all in individuals being systematically and structurally denied basic human needs — not because of an absence of desire, but because life has been ordered in such a way as to isolate and alienate individuals for the political and economic benefit of the few. The perennial question raised by Gustavo Gutiérrez many years ago still speaks volumes, *"How do we tell the poor of this world that God loves them?"*

My intention is to say that the Christian church must make normative the prophetic vision of justice and community, instituted by that first-century Jew, Jesus, and given expression in the lives of figures like Martin Luther King Jr., Desmond Tutu, Mother Teresa, Gandhi, Oscar Romero, and Cesar Chavez. Christian theology must surrender its preoccupation with doing theology in such a way that attempts to justify the current social order; that retreats from direct engagement with the powers and principalities, making social life for many painfully unbearable. This is evident in the renewed interest in suppressing understandings of Christianity that speak to systemic and political transformation.

Even after the courageous and discursive voices of liberation movements of the mid–twentieth century, it is rather appalling that few (if any) within the Western theological establishment are interested in talking about the question of justice, privilege, power, or platitudinous and blatant dimensions of human suffering. With all the talk and criticism about the Enlightenment project, the question that refuses to go away is: What does postmodernity mean for those who suffer? And what should be the Christian response (or that of anyone else)? Approaching this question or not approaching the question is already troubling for a culture determined to police out the recognition of any form of suffering from mind, body, and spirit.

What Prophetic Rage Means for Black Theology

I argue that there are at least five matters that persons concerned with the liberation of black peoples and humanity in general must attend to in this age. First, they must critically appraise the ways in which economic, cultural, and political changes taking place from the late sixties to the present have impacted and/or undermined the black theological agenda. Second, they must come to grips with black theology's unrealized hopes and promises on the backdrop of the reality that the civil rights movement was left incomplete. Although often cast as a sort of triumphalistic historical event that brought forth daybreak from the long night of despair, the civil rights movement, with all its gain, now faces more nuanced and insidious forms of economic and political subjugation. Third, they must address the fact that white theologians, and the broader academy for that matter, never truly embraced the message of black theologians. With a few courageous exceptions such as Frederick Herzog and the poetic dissonance of James Perkinson, black theology has virtually fallen on deaf ears. As black theologians have moved aggressively toward issues of sexuality, pan-Africanist studies, humanism, and ethical methodologies, many of us are compelled to ask if black theology has grown out of touch with the painful and crushing realities of black ghettos, and the malingering conditions leaving many in a position Derrick Bell described as "soul-devastating despair." Bell's piercing cultural appraisal of the black situation post–civil rights is quite illustrative:

> The fact of slavery refuses to fade, along with the deeply embedded personal attitudes and public policy assumptions that supported it for so long. Indeed, the racism that made slavery feasible is far from dead in the last decade of twentieth century America; and the civil rights gains, so hard won, are being steadily eroded. Despite undeniable progress for many, no African Americans are insulated from incidents of racial discrimination. Our careers, even our lives, are threatened because of color. Even the most successful of us are haunted by the plight of our less fortunate brethren who struggle for existence in what some social scientists call the "underclass." Burdened with life-long poverty and soul-devastating despair, they live beyond the pale of the American Dream. What we designate as "racial progress" is not a solution to that problem. It is a regeneration of the problem in a particularly perverse form.[8]

Bell's sentiments are echoed in the reflective and enigmatic words of Albert Raboteau in his spiritual autobiography, *A Sorrowful Joy:* "the pain,

---

8. Derrick Bell, *Faces at the Bottom of the Well: The Permanence of Racism* (New York: Basic Books, 1992), 3.

the injustice, the abuse, and the evil — passing on generation after generation — blind us."[9] Recognizing the persistent reality of suffering in the world, Raboteau is quick to remind us, lest we fall into the nihilistic abyss, that the compassion reflected in God's sustaining and abiding love compels us onward toward freedom and liberation. Raboteau's reflections require us to renew our confrontation with what Walter Wink describes as the social, political, and economic powers and principalities of our day.

Fourth, as I argue in this book, perhaps the only convincing response to the postmodern problem of nihilism, and the systemic forces of economic and political subjugation, is prophetic rage. I do not employ rage in this instance as a pathological or emotional condition, as if one could separate so easily the activities of mind, body, and spirit. Rather, prophetic rage refers to the kind of theological praxis expressed in the life and words of the ancient prophets and the prophetic witnesses of the church like Martin Luther King Jr., Sojourner Truth, Clarence Jordan, Dorothy Day, St. Francis of Assisi, Miguel d'Escoto, Howard Thurman, Dietrich Bonhoeffer, Marian Wright Edelman, Fannie Lou Hamer, and countless others. They were more than simply exemplars of faithful Christian praxis. Through their witness to the church in the quest for justice, human dignity, and freedom for those on the fringes, they offer compelling insights through the vista of human history of God's activity in the world. Modern theology's preoccupation with rationalism and personal autonomy, in distancing theory and praxis, continues to be one of the most imposing barriers to transformative and prophetic Christian witness in the world. However, by listening to the voices and stories, and following the footprints, of those who defeated hopelessness in their own times with prophetic rage and action, I believe we will discover powerfully illuminating pathways to social justice, reconciliation, and faithful witness in our time.

Specifically, J. Kameron Carter's book *Race: A Theological Account* has received a great deal of attention, and creates an extraordinary opportunity for dialogue on the emergence of a new stage of black theology. Carter's theological treatment of race is groundbreaking and offers new insights for understanding black suffering as a basis for prophetic Christianity in the world. Both Carter and I share a deep concern for reclaiming a "countertradition" that may have been disrupted in the saga of modernity. Carter's treatment of figures like Harriet Jacobs, Jarena Lee, and enslaved black bodies as "death-bound subjects" reflects a brilliant critique of the

---

9. Albert Raboteau, *A Sorrowful Joy* (Mahwah, N.J.: Paulist, 2002), 59.

prevailing triumphalism of American evangelicalism. In this sense, Carter's theology, buttressed by the urgent call of prophetic rage, supports the development of a form of prophetic Christianity that challenges empire and indeed the cultural forces of nihilism as well. Prophetic rage insists upon a crucial dialogue with Carter's reading of black theology and race, and the challenges of attending to the persistent and oppressive systems' social, political, and economic injustice. Carter claims the problem of race comes about because of modernity's preoccupation with binary oppositions and western Germanic culture as the apex of human civilization. He argues that by reclaiming the Jewishness of Jesus, thus avoiding the linguistic binary of race (which contributed to the stabilizing narrative of white supremacy and empire in the modern era), there is a way forward to overcome the legacy of race in the postmodern world. Although Carter intends to overcome the problem of race, especially through his meticulous review and critique of modern theological and philosophical discourse and his embrace of the early Church Father Gregory of Nyssa, Carter in fact reinforces and intensifies the reality of empire, white supremacy, and racism in not only his methodology and argumentation, but also in his overall conclusions. Carter blatantly denies the very voices and bodies that have resisted empire through salvation history, women and children, peasants and the poor, widows and orphans, and the enslaved, none of whose voices appear at any point in Carter's volume. The most compelling distinction between *Race: A Theological Account* and *Prophetic Rage* is that the former is situated firmly within the tradition of colonizing theology, a tradition that has helped to promote, sustain, and inflict untold suffering on marginalized voices, while the latter stands at the center of the tradition of liberating theologies, specifically black theologies of liberation, that have fought to dismantle such systems. In Carter's focus on three key figures in African American discourse on the problem of racism (Albert Raboteau, James Cone, and Charles Long, favoring Long more than the other two), he ignores and dismisses the tremendous complexity of the tradition and lived experience as "text," as observed by Emilie Townes; lived experiences of bodies that by their mere refusal to die were able to resist colonizing and imperial theologies that wished to render them silent.

Carter, along with many of his conversation partners (from Stanley Hauerwas, Willie Jennings, and Catherine Pickstock, to Graham Ward and others), calls into question the underlying presuppositions of social theory, of which he suggests black theology (and other theologies of liberation) is a chief benefactor. While challenging classical perspectives on black theology, Carter does provide a refreshing and compelling glimpse into possibilities of constructing a new black theology that is attentive to the pitfalls of modernity and Cone's reliance on Barth's colonial theology from above. Instead, Carter introduces a "postcolonial Barthianism" that views race as fundamentally a theological problem that may be reconciled through critical reflection on the "Jewishness of Jesus." He also argues that those courageous, prophetic, liberating voices (including Cone's) would reach their aims of liberation by reaching back to premodern Augustinian days, where the church might create a new way of being in the world. *Prophetic Rage,* in contrast, points to the ways in which human suffering and the quest for healing, redemption, and justice, in today's global world, serve as perhaps the ultimate and final authority on all life and reality, serving as a lens through which to view the transformative activity of God in the world.

Finally, theologians in general, and black theologians in particular, must go beyond rigid compartmentalization, which has characterized much of the theology produced in Western institutions in modernity and carrying on into the present. Human beings do not live compartmentalized lives, only speaking to, listening to, talking to, and interacting with like fellows. On the contrary, the realities of today create the conditions for a multidimensional, fluid existence where there is a constant exchange of ideas, stories, experiences, theories, disciplines, genres, and methodologies. If Leonardo Boff is correct when he observes that the budding technologically drenched world we now live in is about making "connections," then Christian theologians, churches, and believers must also be about making critical and creative connections to the comprehensive and complex dimensions of the human experience. The human suffering endured by the majority of the world's population today involves making such connections, not least with poor blacks within the American context. Bonhoeffer's prophetic wisdom, written in one of his last letters from Tegel prison in 1944, offers this gripping summary: "Who stands fast? Only the one whose final standard is not his reason, his principles, his conscience, his freedom or his virtue, but the one who is ready to sacrifice all this when he is called to obedient and responsible action in faith and in exclusive allegiance to God — the responsible person, who tries to make his whole life an answer to the question and call of God."[10]

---

10. Dietrich Bonhoeffer, *Letters and Papers from Prison,* cited in *Cloud of Witnesses,* ed. Jim Wallis and Joyce Hollyday (Maryknoll, N.Y.: Orbis, 2005), 264.

CHAPTER ONE

Black Religion and Nihilism

*Love your enemies. . . . Let no man pull you so low as to make
you hate him. . . . If you will protest courageously, and yet with
dignity and Christian love, when the history books are written in
future generations, the historians will have to pause to say
"There lived a great people — a black people — who injected new
meaning and dignity into the veins of civilization." This is our
challenge and our overwhelming responsibility.*[1]

*Let your motto be resistance! resistance! resistance! No oppressed
people have ever secured their liberty without resistance. What
kind of resistance you had better make, you must decide by the
circumstances that surround you, and according to the sugges-
tion of expediency. Brethren, adieu! Trust in the living God. Labor for the peace of the human race, and remember that you are
four millions.*[2]

---

1. Lerone Bennett Jr., *What Manner of Man?* (Chicago: Johnson Publishing Co., 1962),
66. See also C. Eric Lincoln's *Race, Religion, and the Continuing American Dilemma* (New
York: Hill and Wang, 1984), 95.

2. Henry Highland Garnet, "An Address to the Slaves of the United States, Delivered
before the National Convention of Colored Citizens, Buffalo, New York, August 16, 1843,"
published in Henry Highland Garnet, *Walker's Appeal, with a Brief Sketch of His Life. And
also Garnet's Address to the Slaves of the United States of America* (New York: J. H. Tobitt,
1848).

Prophetic rage has signified the power and courage of black people to fight against those very systems that have sought to undermine their very being. Black religion has also played a pivotal role in offering a prophetic critique of the values, beliefs, and rituals that the Western world in general, and America in particular, has held in such high regard when it comes to freedom, justice, human dignity, and the like. Even in the context of the Christian tradition, it was black religion, whether in apartheid South Africa or in the Jim Crow segregation of southern America, that demonstrated the meaning of faithfulness and Christian love. On black religion, C. Eric Lincoln observed that "our strange dilemma is that the human values we hold as individuals are routinely eviscerated by the inhuman systems we create to negate them in our consuming passion to distinguish and separate humans from other humans."[3] Rooted in the painful horrors of slavery and colonialism, black religion (and subsequently black theology) has been marked by a theology of resistance and prophetic protest, paving the way for and in concert with liberationist movements around the world. Even with the election of the nation's first black president (Barack Obama) in 2008, and reelection in 2012, the deep legacy of black religion's struggle with empire remains a constant reminder of its unshakable hope and the challenges that persist as well.

Those challenges and struggles are played out in the geopolitical theater of black life. My own experience as a black boy growing up in the belly of the South is no different. I was raised as part of the post–civil rights generation. The promised land of which Dr. King spoke was not realized and remains evasive. I was born in 1971 and raised in a small wood house in the back hills of Georgia in a lumber town in the deep woods. In the house, I was reared as the only brother of seven sisters. In that little house, life was hard. We were poor and black in the South. Although the systemic and legalized structures of segregation had been dismantled, the forces of racism and segregation were ingrained in the very fabric of southern culture. In the summers, we toiled in tobacco fields in sizzling heat. The world of blackness, my world, was separate and distinct from the outer world. As W. E. B. Du Bois observed in his description of the "veil" in the *Souls of Black Folks*, southern life was still persistently segregated and unequal. I rarely recall even engaging a white person or persons of other cultural groups for much of my early childhood. Although the school system was supposedly integrated, there was segregation in integration. Blacks were

---

3. Lincoln, *Race, Religion*, xii.

segregated in different classrooms and often presented with inferior and subpar resources and educational opportunities. Up until I graduated high school in 1989, my school system and the surrounding counties still held separate proms. Not only was there segregation in school programming, nearly every social, political, and economic institution in the South remained segregated. The churches were segregated. Barbershops, beauty salons, restaurants, and even day-care centers were separate. With the separation came different worlds with often very different rules and norms. Early on when I expressed interest in taking college-bound classes or participating in certain kinds of school activities and encountered resistance, I realized that what was at stake was power and the stabilization of white supremacist ideologies, which were in fact intertwined with the larger forces of empire. Practices of racism and discrimination at the local level are directly linked to larger, wider systems of empire and nihilism. These experiences were simply a microcosm of the challenges faced in black life particularly, and in a much broader sense in the struggles of marginalized persons the world over. Empire and its systems are personal and structural, blatant and subtle, visible and invisible all at once.

The greatest lie and deception of empire is found in the presumed sense of individual agency. Empire, on which white supremacy (and other systems) is dependent, is a narrative that is stabilized and held intact by the guise of personal preference. It is presumed somehow that even within these systems individuals have the ability to exercise their rational capacities and somehow emerge victoriously above these systems if they so desire. In some ways, this thesis holds true. Through reason, personal autonomy, and the power of self-determination it is possible to change and transform one's circumstances and perhaps, in a Niebuhrian sense, to reconfigure societal structures. However, for the masses living in poverty and hopelessness, the odds are not in their favor. The systems themselves, when buttressed by ideologies of white supremacy, patriarchy, heterosexism, and militarism, are designed to advance a particular narrative of cultural normativity, which in turn stabilizes the system. Black life stands at the epicenter and crossroads of modernity, at the intersection of its dream and its nightmare. Black life exposes the myth of reason and enlightenment as the key to progress and moral perfection. In short, the realities of black life and its struggle for hope and redemption have laid out before the Western world its greatest sin — the negation of humanity by humanity. By denying black life, the Western world, America in particular, in some sense denies its own existence and is confronted with the end of its own history.

In the small town of my birth, there were two churches, one Baptist and the other Presbyterian. One church ebbed up from the gallows of poverty and came into being as part of the carpetbagging industries of Reconstruction, rooted in those pseudoforms of slavery and black codes that introduced indentured servitude that lasted more than a hundred years after the Emancipation Proclamation. The other stood in this small, seductively tranquil community, as a symbol of privilege and state power. Members of the two churches never interacted on Sundays, the days of worship, but throughout the week daily in the fields and workhouses as a curious dance of bondage and privilege, friend and foe, slave and free.

On the fiftieth anniversary of the March on Washington, and the sesquicentennial anniversary of the Emancipation Proclamation, critical questions persist as to the ways in which movements for peace, justice, and reconciliation are increasingly challenged by the intensification of conflicts, competing narratives, globalization, and most notably the problem of difference and pluralism. Indeed, for oppressed peoples the world over, postmodernity comes not merely as a philosophical problem but as a material and social crisis of hope and survival. Black people, in particular, are suffering like never before. In spite of all the hype about the black middle class, and public images of celebrities like Oprah Winfrey, Jay-Z, Chris Rock, and the fabulous life of Sean "P. Diddy" Combs, the drowning sense of hopelessness and despair overtaking many poor urban and rural communities alike makes postmodernity appear as not just the end of "meaning" but as the end of "existence." Literally, where do we go from here? Experience has shown that the economic, political, and intellectual structures of modernity militate against black existence. Hence, what seems to be called for is a reassessment of the social, theological, and philosophical systems that have been taken for granted in the lives of black folks, and assumed as fact in black theology and European and American theological discourse in general.

Nihilism and Black Theology

If black theology, in its current state, is not dead, it is certainly on life support. As a movement, black theology remains, on the one hand, one of the most powerful theological inventions of the twentieth century inasmuch as it spoke to the very core of white supremacist ideologies, Western imperialism, and the broader plight of the poor and dispossessed in the West and globally. On the other hand, with its institutionalization and reliance on modern theological presuppositions and lack of critical, sustained engagement with the black church and praxis, black theology as a movement is suffering from the drumbeat of prophetic zeal. Before putting forth a prophetic vision of black theology that incorporates both postmodern and postcolonial critiques, we must as a point of departure briefly assess the development, shifts, and trends in black theology.

Nihilism: The Greatest Threat to Black Survival

The developments and emerging trends in black theology are unintelligible apart from the current threat of nihilism. Nihilism has always been the greatest enemy of oppressed peoples. Black theology has devoted much of its attention to dismantling white supremacy in theology. But white supremacy has never been the greatest enemy of black people. That enemy has appeared again and again in the form of a deadly dance with hopelessness, lovelessness, and despair. Nihilism, historically and today, has been the greatest and most crushing foe of the survival and thriving of black life in America and through the African diaspora. For enslaved and colonized peoples, as well as those bodies gripped by the entangled beast of patriarchy and heterosexism, nihilism, the reality of hopelessness, is what kills the will to fight. Without hope, there is no struggle. Without hope, there is no resistance. Without hope, there is no future. Nihilism appears as the invisible force that robs oppressed people of the desire and courage to organize, strategize, and mobilize to envision new realities. It comes as acquiescence to present systems, as silence to the status quo in the face of injustice. Nihilism, emerging from the ancient thrust of empire as the will to power, to control, to dominate, and to define reality for all human beings, is what steals the very desire and impulse for survival and life. As Cornel West observed, nihilism is "a natural consequence of a culture (or civilization) ruled and regulated by categories that mask manipulation, mastery and domination of peoples and nature." In short, as West reminds us, "the faith in the categories of reason is the cause of nihilism."[4] Maurice Blanchot offers a compelling summation of nihilism: "The moment Nihilism outlines the world for us, its counterpart, science, creates the tools to dominate it. The era of universal mastery is opened. But there are some consequences:

4. *The Cornel West Reader* (New York: Basic Civitas Books, 1999), 208.

21

first, science can only be nihilistic; it is the meaning of a world deprived of meaning, a knowledge that ultimately has ignorance as its foundation. . . . Nihilism becomes the possibility of science — which means that the human world can be destroyed by it."[5]

I have seen this nihilism up close in my own experience. For most of my childhood, I lived a relatively quiet existence in a small country house in a little town called McGregor, Georgia, on the edge of what was once a slave plantation. Winters were cold then and summers were blistering hot. I recall very early on observing the deep hardship and pain of black life. There was a small store in town, owned by the family who lived in the "big house" with big trees. The store allowed the few who lived in the community to purchase staples like milk, flour, and bread. Many of the people who frequented the store also worked for the store owner and were allowed a line of credit for such goods. My family lived about two miles from the store, and occasionally we would walk to the store to pick up what we needed. On the walk to the store one day with my father, I walked by a small, deep crimson, shotgun house. It was very small, with barely enough room for one person. I entered the house with my father. There was no running water or electricity. An old potbelly stove sat in the middle of the floor with a silver pipe protruding from its head to a hole in the ceiling. There stood an old man in the house, stooped over, as if carrying a heavy load. His face was dark and weathered. He looked tired but fully awake. His hands were withered and his voice was like sound breaking through shattered glass on his tonsils. It seemed as if his soul was weary. My father reminded me that he worked for the landowner his entire life. After a brief and pleasant exchange, we prepared to leave. As we looked toward the door, he reached deep in his pocket and pulled out the shiniest coin I had ever seen. It was a half-dollar. What I had seen in the face of this old man was the face of nihilism and its bitter defeat. I had seen the weight of empire and the hope that makes empires tremble. I had seen at once death and life in one fragile, withered body. It was indeed the tragedy and triumph of modern philosophy and the prophetic determination of resistance and hope, of the refusal to die, give up, give in, and give out.

American and European philosophers, in their preoccupation with distinctions and categories, from Richard Rorty, Jürgen Habermas, Gilles

---

5. Maurice Blanchot, "The Limits of Experience: Nihilism," in *The New Nietzsche: Contemporary Styles of Interpretation,* edited and introduced by David B. Allison (New York, 1977), 122-23, in *The Cornel West Reader,* 209.

Deleuze, Paul Ricoeur, W. V. O. Quine, Thomas Kuhn, and Larry Rasmussen, to Jacques Derrida, are victims of nihilism's destructive tendencies even as they resist its seductive lure. These viewpoints result in a sophisticated and complex matrix of meaninglessness that erupts over into a culture of lifelessness, lovelessness, and despair. It has been this meaninglessness that, since the days of slavery colonialism, black bodies have resisted and contested.

Black theology, in its curious reflection on black life, has sought to articulate God-talk and God-thought as a response to the nihilistic threat. Black theology is multidimensional. It incorporates a multitude of voices, theological perspectives, ideas, methodologies, disciplines, cultures, and experiences. Black theology is "an effort of African American people to claim their blackness and their freedom as people of God."[6] As it has done in the past, black theology within a postmodern and postcolonial context must engage a multitude of approaches and perspectives in order to gain a richer understanding of black life and the meaning of liberation. Although black theology is rooted within the field of theology, it must not be limited by it. In the early stages of black theology and throughout its development, it has reflected many voices, representing a symphony of voices calling for the freedom of black people in multiple forms.

Since a group of "Negro churchmen" published a statement on black power in the *New York Times* on July 31, 1966, a critical debate emerged and continues into the present, as to what theology (in general) and the black church (in particular) have to say to the weak and powerless, to those struggling with their "backs against the wall."[7] Several figures such as Gayraud Wilmore, C. Eric Lincoln, Cecil Cone, Major Jones, Charles Long, J. Deotis Roberts, James Cone, Albert Cleage, Jacquelyn Grant, Katie Geneva Cannon, Delores Williams, Renita Weems, Charles Copher, and Marcia Riggs represent those distinctive voices that helped to establish the context out of which current debates are taking place.[8] Close attention to

---

6. Dwight N. Hopkins, *Introducing Black Theology of Liberation* (Maryknoll, N.Y.: Orbis, 1999), 4.

7. Howard Thurman, *Jesus and the Disinherited* (reprint, Boston: Beacon Press, 1996).

8. Other major proponents in establishing foundations for black theology include (but are not limited to): Mark Chapman, Paul Garber, Vincent Harding, William R. Jones, Richard McKinney, Henry H. Mitchell, Preston N. Williams, Charles Shelby Rooks, Robert C. Williams, Allan Boesak, John Mbiti, Joseph A. Johnson, James Gardiner, Lawrence E. Lucas, Kelly Brown Douglas, JoAnne Terrell, Priscilla Massie, Basil Moore, Olin Moyd, Albert Raboteau, Joseph Washington, and Nathan Wright.

the theological tensions between Cone and Roberts, as well as their later works, however, provides a helpful entry point into the relationship between black theology and postmodernity, and postcolonialism.

Cone's *Black Theology and Black Power* represents his most radical assault on white supremacist hegemonic influences in Western theology and the ways in which they reinforce systems and structures that militate against black freedom.[9] His later works, *A Black Theology of Liberation, God of the Oppressed,* and *Black Theology: A Documentary History* (volumes 1 and 2), advanced his core theological argument that the very nature of the Christian narrative is liberation of the poor and oppressed. In these texts, Cone was attempting to address charges that black theology was simply social theory in *guise.* His other works, *The Emergence of a Black Theology of Liberation, Speaking Truth to Power: Ecumenism, Liberation, and Black Theology, For My People: Black Theology and the Black Church,* and *My Soul Looks Back,* particularly emphasized the context of the black church and dialogue with other oppressed groups (in addition to the black poor) as necessary elements of black theology.[10] Cone's *The Spirituals and the Blues,* which has received much less attention than his other works, is perhaps the most promising as a resource for doing black theology in a postmodern framework precisely because in this text Cone identifies the spirituals and blues music as *theological texts* for doing black theology. Whereas Cone drew heavily on Barthian theology and neoorthodoxy to establish the basis and legitimacy of black theology in earlier works, his interpretation of the spirituals and blues in the black experience points to both the complexity and the fluidity of the black experience with suffering

---

9. James H. Cone, *Black Theology and Black Power* (New York: Seabury Press, 1969). See also Cone's "Black Consciousness and the Black Church," *Christianity and Crisis* 30 (November 2 and 16, 1970): 244-50, and his "Christianity and Black Power," in *Is Anybody Listening to Black America?* ed. C. Eric Lincoln (New York: Seabury Press, 1968), 3-9.

10. Here, I wish to simply offer a general appraisal of Cone's work so that I can later point out both the strengths and weaknesses of black theology in Cone and Roberts for the purpose of appropriating various elements within a postmodern and postcolonial framework. See the following: James H. Cone, *Risks of Faith: The Emergence of a Black Theology of Liberation, 1968-1998* (Boston: Beacon Press, 1999); *A Black Theology of Liberation,* 20th anniversary ed. (Maryknoll, N.Y.: Orbis, 1990); *Black Theology: A Documentary History,* 2nd ed. (Maryknoll, N.Y.: Orbis, 1993); *For My People: Black Theology and the Black Church; Where Have We Been and Where Are We Going?* (Maryknoll, N.Y.: Orbis, 1984); *Speaking the Truth: Ecumenism, Liberation, and Black Theology* (Grand Rapids: Eerdmans, 1986); *The Spirituals and the Blues: An Interpretation* (New York: Seabury Press, 1972); and *Martin and Malcolm and America: A Dream or a Nightmare* (Maryknoll, N.Y.: Orbis, 2000).

as opposed to other works that seem to marginalize and fragment the multiple dimensions of black life. Even his most recent book, *The Cross and the Lynching Tree,* has remained astoundingly consistent with his earlier works in maintaining that white supremacy still represents the greatest challenge to the church's witness in the West and that the ability of white Christians to connect lynching to the cross holds the key to Christian faithfulness in America and the Western world.

Cone's lack of attention to the realities of empire leaves much to be desired, however. The fact that blacks have been victimized by the forces of white supremacy historically and into the present, as Cone argues, holds true, but he overlooks the ways in which blacks have at times been complicit in the totalizing power of empire, particularly as it relates to systems of patriarchy and the American caste system. For instance, while Cone rightfully decries the problem of white supremacy in classical and contemporary Christian theology, the very institutions and systems through which he shares his message of protest directly support, reinforce, and empower systems of domination and exploitation. Cone's quandary is that his very critique and involvement in the "academy" have become in part the blood fuel for empire. Cone's analysis of white supremacy and the racism in Christian theology would be greatly advanced if he also began to challenge empire and the embedded capitalistic forces at work in the intellectual and academic enterprise. For instance, many endowment-driven academic institutions, with their hedge funds, global finance portfolios, and Wall Street investments, find themselves complicit in the death-dealing work of empire, if only by association. Any critique of white supremacy that does not take into account the larger systemic forces of empire and global capitalism that hold blacks and whites in its sway, is profoundly incomplete and shortsighted. I will say more about this in subsequent chapters.

As a student at Morehouse College in the 1990s, I knew nothing of Cone or the black theology movement. It was a season of discovery and popularized revolt. The Rodney King beatings and the L.A. riots set off a firestorm of new rage that erupted in urban centers across the nation. Public Enemy's famous "Fight the Power" song along with the provocative and controversial young group NWA (Niggas with Attitude) were ahistorical treatments of the conditions of blacks in urban settings saturated with drugs, alcohol, police brutality, violence, and broken families. During this period, the city of Atlanta was a hotbed of megachurches. Eddie L. Long's New Birth Baptist Church exploded on the scene as well. It was as if the church had virtually ignored James Cone's interpretation of black theology; his zealous critique of white supremacy seemed to be directed at the white church in a search for black respectability and legitimation, not to the black masses crying out for hope and a pathway to freedom. At a moment when black theology had in a real sense come full circle and was maturing as a field of study, it remained extraordinarily aloof from the everyday struggles of black life. It attended to many things, but nihilism among urban black youth did not seem to be one of them.

So, during a talk by a seminary student at a session at the Martin Luther King Jr. International Chapel, for the first time I heard of J. Deotis Roberts and black theology. I was an eager listener. For years I had sought to reconcile my evangelical roots of soul salvation with my hunger for justice and social transformation. I treasured my connection to the church and a personal understanding of God on the one hand, and my connection to the revolutionary ideas of W. E. B. Du Bois, Walt Whitman, Martin Luther King Jr., and Karl Marx on the other. The seminary student talked about a field of theology that was concerned with reflecting on black life and black freedom. He discussed Roberts's *Liberation and Reconciliation;* Roberts was at that time a professor at Eastern Baptist Theological Seminary, where the student was enrolled. I immediately became absorbed in what would become a lifelong passion.

A few days later, I wrote to Roberts requesting to study with him, asking him to consider taking me under his tutelage. He promptly wrote back agreeing to such a relationship. Like Cone, Roberts thickened the analysis of black theology by bringing it into dialogue with classical historical theological discourse relating to the doctrine of God, theological anthropology, and reconciliation. Carter's theology of race would be further enhanced through a critical reflection of the theology of J. Deotis Roberts, who is steeped in the classical historical theological tradition of D. M. Baile. Cone offers a very one-dimensional perspective of black theology. However, Roberts's theology is to a large extent in dialogue with the Western philosophical and theological tradition. By expanding his reading of black theology in Roberts and other voices like Major Jones and William R. Jones, Carter would strengthen his assessment of black theology as he seeks to reclaim a counternarrative of the Christian tradition. Roberts was shaped in philosophical theology nearly a decade before Cone. An ordained Baptist minister from Tarboro, North Carolina, Roberts published two very important texts: *From Puritanism to Platonism in Seventeenth Century England* and *Faith and Reason: A Comparative Study of Pascal, Bergson, and James.*[11]

---

11. J. Deotis Roberts, *From Puritanism to Platonism in Seventh Century England* (The

From Puritanism to Platonism was the first serious treatment of the life and thought of Benjamin Whichcote, father of Cambridge Platonism. At the height of seventeenth-century humanism at Cambridge University, Whichcote, according to Roberts, was able to firmly situate the Puritan understanding of the Christian faith with a recovery of Platonism.

In *Faith and Reason,* one sees a young Roberts struggling with the theological and methodological tensions of the Christian faith on what it means to be both a critical thinker and a person of faith. Here, Roberts actually anticipates Carter's and Cornel West's concern with binary oppositions and situates the problem in terms of the much deeper issue of the limits of reason itself. In short, Roberts was pursuing the question, as Howard Thurman observed, of how to love God with both "head and heart." He would go on to agree with Pascal's declaration that "the heart has reasons the mind cannot understand." Regarding Carter's critique of black theology in *Race: A Theological Account,* Roberts raises the simplistic question of where the critique emerges, from within or from without? In other words, Roberts's overall assertion has to do with the very questions we ask. He observes that Carter's conclusions, as well as his general critiques of black theology, are rendered suspect by his authoritative sources, and lack of critical engagement with the tradition itself.[12]

Roberts's critical response to Cone's indictment of the classical American theological enterprise was *Liberation and Reconciliation,* published in 1971.[13] Here, Roberts argued that indeed the essence of the gospel is liberation of the oppressed, that God is in fact on the side of black people in their quest for justice and human dignity. Roberts also affirmed that the kind of liberation the gospel renders is a reconciling liberation, or rather, liberation that finds its end and fulfillment in a just and loving community reconciled with both God and neighbor. Roberts's *Black Political Theology* and *Black Theology in Dialogue* were specific efforts to claim a more universal tenor to the essential claims of black theology. In both texts, Roberts argued that black theology as a theological movement sought to liberate poor blacks from the systemic realities of white racism in America; indeed, it sought to liberate all people — including whites. In *Black Theology in Di-*

Hague: Martinus Nijhoff, 1968), and *Faith and Reason: A Comparative Study of Pascal, Bergson, and James* (Boston: Christopher Publishing House, 1962).

12. Interview with J. Deotis Roberts by Johnny Bernard Hill, at the home of Roberts in Bowie, Maryland, circa 2010.

13. J. Deotis Roberts, *Liberation and Reconciliation: A Black Theology* (Maryknoll, N.Y.: Orbis, 1971; originally published by Westminster Press).

alogue, Roberts made the specific case for black theology, and more broadly oppressed communities from around the world, to establish a critical dialogue. Here, his understanding of black theology, as a theology of liberation for the oppressed, was in dialogue with adherents of *minjung* theology, black feminists, believers of Latin American liberation theologies, black Catholics, and representatives from world religions.

Roberts and I shared much in common. Both of us emerged out of the South; we were both Baptists. Both he and I also suffered great losses, which seemed to sensitize us to the deep perennial question of human suffering and theodicy. Roberts suffered the loss of his son, J. Deotis Roberts Jr., in a traffic accident when he was only nineteen years old. I experienced the loss of my mother (of whom I am named) in a vehicle accident when I was just thirteen years old. At nineteen years old, I received the call of my father's death from complications related to alcoholism, a far too common predicament in oppressed communities.

Roberts's work has, in sum, been multidimensional and interdisciplinary, and offers a postcolonial critique of modern theology and philosophy by refusing to remain landlocked in any particular category of study. Roberts also directed his attention toward connecting black theology to the ministry of black churches, particularly later in his career. His later works, such as *Roots of the Black Future: Family and Church, The Prophethood of Black Believers: An African American Political Theology for Ministry,* and *Africentric Christianity: A Theological Appraisal for Ministry,* all reflect a sort of disenchantment with the often detached, elitist, and exclusionary impulse of the academy. Each text, though rigorous in theological reflection, is deeply concerned with appropriating theological discourse as praxis for empowering creative social transformation in churches and society.

In some sense, Roberts's later works and Cone's emphasis on connecting black theology with the spirituals and the blues express the need for black theology to continue its insistence on both theory and praxis, or what Cone calls "ortho-praxis." Cone and Roberts, as well as other major proponents of black theology in its initial stages in the early 1970s, recognized that one of its major pitfalls was its lack of ongoing engagement (in both thought and practice) with the black church and poor black people. Black theology became institutionalized, in some sense cut off and alienated from the masses of poor black people and ghettos in urban centers around the world. Black theology, instead of speaking to, with, and for black people, became preoccupied with legitimization and the concerns of methodology.

In recent years, black theology (like Latin American liberation theologies) has been essentially written off by much of the academic community as an essential conversation partner in critical reflection on the Christian narrative. On the one hand, there is no need in wasting time answering critiques of liberation theologies because the motives and systems of thought still proceed out of an imperialist, colonialist worldview that seems incapable of dialogue with other ways of thinking beyond the Eurocentric context. In short, why should black theology spend time engaging the nuances and methodologies of colonizing, Western constructions of theology?

On the other hand, the fact remains that black theology is being done in a persistent context of white supremacist social, political, and even theological structures. Many of the social institutions that determine the public lives of the vast majority of black people in American society are controlled by whites. With all the black wealth put together, blacks still hold less than one-half of 1 percent of the nation's wealth. The dramatic disparities in wealth also translate into a sort of political paralysis of black progress. Poverty, housing, incarceration, and education are areas that continue to stall black flourishing. But this is not unrelated to the ways in which local churches, denominational officials, seminaries, and theological educators do business. The same CEOs, judges, politicians, bank managers, wardens, and police officers who may contribute to the further derailment of black flourishing also tend to be active members and participants in ecclesiological circles, informing the very ideas, systems, and structures that theological ideas inhabit. So, it is imperative for black theology, as a relevant and contextual discipline, to not only engage postmodern and postcolonial discourse but also to take up the task of deconstructing its very origins in the process of reconstructing a black theology that speaks to a postmodern age.

Roberts and Cone, as with many of their generation, touted the black struggle against systemic racism and white supremacy in America while failing to see the particular struggle of black women as they resisted both white supremacy and gender inequalities. Drawing on the work of James Cone, Jacquelyn Grant and Delores Williams were pioneers in casting a prophetic theological vision of doing theology and ethics. Stephanie Mitchem describes womanist theology as "the systematic, faith-based exploration of the many facets of African American women's religiosity."[14]

---

14. Stephanie Y. Mitchem, *Introducing Womanist Theology* (Maryknoll, N.Y.: Orbis, 2006), ix. See also Alice Walker's *In Search of Our Mothers' Gardens* (San Diego: Harcourt Brace Jovanovich, 1983).

Womanist theology, she says, is "based on the complex realities of black women's lives. Womanist scholars recognize and name the imagination and initiative that African American women have utilized in developing sophisticated religious responses to their lives."[15]

Resisting Empire: Black Theology, Black Religion, and the Enslaved

The black theology project must be properly situated within the context of the broader religious contours of American evangelical Protestantism and the black experience. These contours express themselves in several areas. Hopkins identifies two essential ingredients that have shaped the development of black theology — the historical context of slavery and the uniqueness of biblical interpretation.[16] Both ingredients have characterized the nature and objectives of the black theology project, and continue to inform them into the present. The latter involves a hermeneutic of resistance. Enslaved Africans incorporated an orientation of an African religious heritage of resistance, endurance, and sociality.

Conversion for early-enslaved Africans meant much more than escape from eternal damnation. It was also a mechanism of survival and eternal redemption. It meant discovering a source of spiritual renewal, inspiration, and hope in the face of racial domination. Embracing Christianity involved a reinterpretation of God from a deistic sustainer of oppression to one who issues a prophetic call to resistance and freedom. What emerged out of the black religious experience with slavery was a distinctively new "black religion." For Gayraud S. Wilmore, "the religious beliefs and rituals of a people are inevitably and inseparably bound up with the material and psychological realities of their daily existence."[17] Throughout the African American religious experience, there has been a sense in which interpreting both who God is and what God is doing has been intimately associated with social experiences. That is to say, understanding and interpreting the Christian faith occur through the lens of concrete social and historical realities. Hence, such distinctions as sacred/secular are

---

15. Mitchem, *Introducing Womanist Theology*, ix.

16. Hopkins, *Introducing Black Theology*, 15ff.

17. Gayraud S. Wilmore, *Black Religion and Black Radicalism: An Interpretation of the Religious History of African Americans*, 3rd ed. (Maryknoll, N.Y.: Orbis, 1998), 22.

of little value since God's work of liberation and love has no boundaries. Within the black religious experience is an assumed critique of a theological tradition that has defended both slavery and black oppression throughout history on theological grounds. Cotton Mather, George Whitefield, and Thomas Bacon were among the chief proponents of a teaching that blacks ordained by God to a life of servitude and slavery was a legitimate form of social ordering.[18]

In slave religion, the question of the existence of God was presupposed. Slavers recognized and affirmed the existence of God prior to exposure to slave captives. The critical question for enslaved Africans, which ran concurrently throughout the African American experience, was whether God suffered with them and in solidarity in their quest for freedom.[19] Questions about God and Jesus Christ were not concerned with rational discourse or preservation of personal autonomy. They took on a more pragmatic quality, or what Emilie Townes describes as a kind of "practical wisdom," by first reflecting on the concrete social situation, often voiced in the spirituals, black preaching, the church, worship, eating, signified storytelling, and broadly speaking, black loving and living. Classical theological themes and the Christian narrative were not only inaccessible because illiteracy was used as a mechanism of social control, but they were also insignificant when contrasted with the daily experience of degradation and brutality.

In particular, the earthly life of Jesus represented divine fellowship in the enslaved African's suffering. Jesus was viewed as an extension of the Old Testament prophetic call for divine justice and the declaration of God's judgment upon the human condition. Theological perspectives on Jesus begin with critical reflection on the black experience. For Cone, a distinction must be made between the Jesus Christ of the Bible and the ways in which Jesus was presented by white missionaries and through such parareligious organizations as the Ku Klux Klan and White Citizens Council. In his book *God of the Oppressed*, Cone says: "where human beings struggle for freedom and refuse to be defined by unauthorized earthly authorities, there Jesus Christ is present among them. His presence is the sus-

---

18. Cited in James Cone, *God of the Oppressed* (Maryknoll, N.Y.: Orbis, 1979); H. Shelton Smith, *In His Image, But . . . : Racism in Southern Religion, 1780-1910* (Durham, N.C.: Duke University Press, 1972), 6f. Cf. also Gilbert Osofsky, *The Burden of Race* (New York: Harper Torchbooks, 1968), 35-44.

19. Cone, *God of the Oppressed*, 50.

taining and liberating event in the lives of the oppressed that makes possible the continued struggle for freedom."[20]

From this point of view, the person of Jesus Christ becomes interdependent with the plight of the oppressed in general, and the experience of black people in particular. According to Cone, "because liberation is God's work of salvation in Jesus Christ, its source and meaning cannot be separated from Christology's sources (Scripture, tradition, and social existence) and content (Jesus in his past, present, and future)."[21] Liberation is cast as a divine gift that flows in and through Jesus Christ, who is at the center of the "project of freedom." "God is the God of Jesus Christ who calls the helpless and weak into a newly created existence. God not only fights for them but takes their humiliated condition upon the divine Person and thereby breaks open a new future for the poor, different from their past and present miseries."[22]

The biblical proclamation of salvation in this sense means liberation for the oppressed. Broadly speaking, a black theology of liberation says that salvation is liberation. There is no soul salvation without social and political liberation from systems of power and domination that crush the soul and spirit. The meaning of the cross is seen in the capacity for Jesus Christ to both identify with black suffering and abandonment (as seen in the Markan passage "My God, my God, why hast thou forsaken me?" [15:34]), and champion the cause of freedom and liberation. Jesus Christ is the fulfillment and promise of freedom and embodies a message of eschatological hope, not only for the future but also in the present.

Prophetic Rage: Black Theology, Postmodernity, and Postcolonialism

Since John Milbank's classic work *Theology and Social Theory,* which called into question many of the presuppositions and methodologies of liberation theologies, and Jean-François Lyotard's *Postmodern Condition: A Report on Knowledge,* a serious dialogue has emerged on the manner in which theology responds to social issues, from war and peace to poverty and racism. In this debate, very little has been said about the connections

20. Cone, *God of the Oppressed,* 32.
21. Cone, *God of the Oppressed,* 127.
22. Cone, *God of the Oppressed,* 128.

between the theological and ethical dimensions of the discussion, and social movements. Cornel West's book *Prophesy Deliverance! An Afro-American Revolutionary Christianity* has made a constructive theological and philosophical attempt to address this area. His two-part series, *Beyond Eurocentrism and Multiculturalism,* and his work *Prophetic Fragments* offer a major critique of the binary linguistic system of Western theological and philosophical discourse.[23] In these writings, West delineates the particular nihilistic tendencies of modern philosophy and theology, pointing instead to the "Afro-American" experience within and beyond the crucible of suffering as an illustration of the most redeemable aspects of postmodern consciousness.

Black theology responded to the problem of white supremacy and empire as an invisible force dominating Christian thought in the West. For instance, the prominence of Western hegemony in theological discourse is observable in that most of the theology coming out of the West in the last two centuries has been written almost exclusively in English, French, Latin, and German. Modern presuppositions arising out of the Enlightenment assumed certain Cartesian and Kantian modes of rationalization and individual autonomy. A hierarchical structure was advanced that situated blackness as antithetical to whiteness, particularly German culture. The "binary linguistic" system guided the formulation of distinctions and categories where whiteness was equated with the good and righteous and blackness was cast as its negation. West, in the essay "Genealogy of Race and Modernity" in *Prophesy Deliverance!,* pursues the deconstructive task by questioning the ways in which race emerged as a theological, social, and linguistic construct. According to West, the problem with theological and philosophical discourse that arose out of modernity lies in its obsession with categories and distinctions reflected in the binary linguistic system that led to a naming of individuals, groups, and geographic locales. In these delineations, Western culture, particularly in Germany, was consid-

23. Cornel West, *Beyond Eurocentrism and Multiculturalism,* vol. 1, *Prophetic Thought in Postmodern Times,* vol. 2, *Prophetic Reflections: Notes on Race and Power in America* (Monroe, Maine: Common Courage Press, 1993); *Prophetic Fragments* (Grand Rapids: Eerdmans, 1988). See also Harvey Cox, *Religion in the Secular City* (New York: Simon and Schuster, 1984); Todd Gitlin, "Hip Deep in Post-Modernism," *New York Times Book Review,* November 6, 1988, 1-36; Jürgen Habermas, "Modernity — an Incomplete Project," in *The Anti-Aesthetic: Essays on Postmodern Culture,* ed. Hal Foster (Port Townsend, Wash.: Bay Press), 3-15; and Charles Long, *Significations: Signs, Symbols, and Images in the Interpretation of Religion* (Philadelphia: Fortress, 1986).

ered the culmination of human development. What emerged was a "degradation of blackness" as the normative theological and philosophical position that went unquestioned until the rise of the abolitionist movement, first in Britain, then in America. These presuppositions continue to reinforce white, colonial, and Western normativity in theological discourse, and thus ongoing fortification of those systems and institutions that militate against black life in particular and human freedom in particular.

In the early nineteenth century, Hegel's groundbreaking work *Philosophy of History* was perhaps the first anthropological text that attended to the historical and cultural aspects of racial and ethnic differences. In it Hegel cast Africa as the "dark continent" of the vast unknown, devoid of history and rational capacities and therefore less than human. A similar characterization was given to what he called the Oriental or Eastern world. The significance of Hegel's thought is seen in his ability to name entire groups and cultures, on philosophical grounds, as less than human. These basic presuppositions are what informed such structures as institutional slavery in America and the subsequent imperialism coming out of the Berlin Conference of 1885, which marked the decisive and formalized beginnings of Western colonialism, particularly in relation to the African continent. An example of this type of thinking was seen in the 1846 *Dred Scott* decision about an African American who lived on free soil for many years and returned to Missouri (a slaveholding state) with a former master who later died.[24] The case simply intensified the tension between slaveholding states and free states, thus hastening the coming of the Civil War. As we will see later, postcolonial discourse seeks to disrupt, subvert, and undermine the debilitating forces of modern theology and its inescapable legacy within postmodern discourse as well.

James Evans, Will Coleman, Dwight Hopkins, Victor Anderson, Monica Coleman, Anthony Pinn, Juan Floyd Thomas, Josiah Young, and Stephen Ray represent the various trajectories of recent attempts at a postmodern dialogue with black theology.[25] Evans's essay "African American

---

24. http://www.historyplace.com/lincoln/dred.htm.

25. This essay does not provide the space for a close examination of these voices. They do represent the various strands of black theology in a contemporary context. For instance, Victor Anderson's *Beyond Ontological Blackness: An Essay on African American Religious and Cultural Criticism* (New York: Continuum, 1995) challenges traditional conversations about race and cultural criticism, accepting the beauty and dignity of black life as a given, and casts a vision of black life as a mosaic or tapestry of resistance, resilience, and human creativity. Both Anthony Pinn and Juan Floyd Thomas attempt to situate black theology as

Christianity and the Postmodern Condition" positions African American Christianity (and black religion in general) as distinctively "postmodern" in character.[26] "One of the peculiar characteristics of black religion has historically been its *difference*, its *alterity*, the way in which it appears to be so strangely ill at ease in the modern world," he writes. By surveying the various dimensions of black life, from the spirituals to African American literature, liturgical practices, and narratives, he posits African American Christianity as an expression of the postmodern mood inasmuch as it has stood "within yet outside of the discursive arena of European-American Christianity, preferring to concern itself with the practical dimensions of its life, and taking for granted its own theological legitimacy."[27] Similarly, Will Coleman, as part of an obscure movement known as the Black Theology Forum, in his essay "Tribal Talk: Black Theology in Postmodern Configurations," introduces a methodological approach to doing black theology that emphasizes collaborative cooperation through dialogue.[28] Doing black theology in a postmodern framework, they insist, requires a radical recovery of African American folk religion, particularly "slave theology," as a way of navigating the nihilistic and fragmenting environment of European-American theological discourse. *Cut Loose Your Stammering Tongue: Black Theology in the Slave Narratives*, edited by Dwight Hopkins and George Cummings, emerged out of those conversations.[29]

These scholars stressed the need to enlist indigenous (and to some ex-

---

humanism. Monica Coleman's recent work, *Making a Way Out of No Way: A Womanist Theology* (Minneapolis: Augsburg Fortress, 2008), is perhaps the first serious constructive theological treatment of womanism and postmodernity. Stephen Ray attends to a reformed doctrinal interpretation of black life and human suffering. His first book, *Do No Harm: Social Sin and Human Responsibility*, serves as a critique of the classical doctrine of sin as narrowly individualistic in scope, and insists on an interpretation of the doctrine of sin as personal and "social" in orientation. J. Kameron Carter's *Race: A Theological Account* (Oxford: Oxford University Press, 2008) does not necessarily fall within the scope of black theology because his work follows in the vein of Radical Orthodoxy and Milbank's critique of liberation theologies.

26. James H. Evans Jr., "African American Christianity and the Postmodern Condition," *Journal of the American Academy of Religion* 58, no. 2 (Summer 1990).

27. Evans, "African American Christianity," 218. See also Gayraud Wilmore, *Black Religion and Black Radicalism: An Interpretation of the Religious History of African Americans*, 2nd ed. (Maryknoll, N.Y.: Orbis, 1983), 11.

28. Will Coleman, "Tribal Talk: Black Theology in Postmodern Configurations," *Theology Today* 50, no. 1 (April 1993): 68-77.

29. Dwight Hopkins and George Cummings, eds., *Cut Loose Your Stammering Tongue: Black Theology in the Slave Narratives* (Maryknoll, N.Y.: Orbis, 1991).

tent, premodern) sources, the experience of black women through womanist theology, and to embrace multidimensional, multilayered theological modes of reflection and analysis. I agree with their central argument that the task of black theology in a pluralistic, incredulous, cultural, and theological context is to "research the religious past of their people for expressions of faith that may be translated into the present."[30] Specifically, slave religion should serve as the primary point of departure for constructing a black theology of liberation for black life today. In a sense they are affirming the African proverbial saying that "only by looking back can we truly move forward." I would also like to suggest that doing black theology in a postmodern context must radically reclaim the prophetic edge in slave religion, the larger black experience, as well as the historical remnants of prophetic Christianity.

Hopkins, in *Liberation Theologies, Postmodernity, and the Americas,* offers a fitting description of postmodernity as it relates to black theology in the USA.

> The Western modern condition for African Americans translated into a metanarrative of white superiority, cogently signified in the adage that a black person (whether slave or free) had no rights that a white man was bound to respect. What was universal, as European modernity crossed the Atlantic and became Euro-American, was that ebony people suffered deleterious asymmetry on a hierarchical scale biologically, theologically, noetically, and culturally. Black slaves knew intuitively that the supposed neutrality of language, trumpeted by the European Enlightenment, could get you killed. What a slave said or did not say vis-à-vis the dominant colonial and subsequent American masters was a matter of life and death. Thus while Europe and Euro-America hailed the rise of modern sensibilities, enlightened epistemologies, and capitalist democracy, Africans and African Americans were already suffering and enduring characteristics of what intellectuals and cultural workers today call postmodernity — such as decentered subjects, multiple locatedness, particularized struggles, no discrepancy between scientific and fictionalized discourse, an impression of the affective and the scientific, the sensuousness of the body and the intellect, and so forth.[31]

30. Will Coleman, "Tribal Talk," 75.

31. David Batstone, Eduardo Mendieta, Lois Ann Lorentzen, and Dwight Hopkins, *Liberation Theologies, Postmodernity, and the Americas* (New York: Routledge, 1997), 207.

Hopkins demonstrates the ways in which black slaves in the courageous resistance to the "negation of blackness" felt the destructive tendencies of modernity long before it appeared as a linguistic critique in recent years. Many postmodern thinkers (especially Derrida, Lyotard, Milbank, and West) have paid special attention to the inherited metaphysical linguistic structures and to developing alternative modalities of discourse capable of "overcoming" the problems posed by modern discourse. Reinvigorating the prophetic dynamics of Christian witness requires a paradigm that challenges the linguistic pitfalls of modernity, while taking seriously the experiences of the dispossessed and marginalized. From this perspective, prophetic rage reflects the impulse to do black theology with the kind of desperate, life-and-death spirit of resistance that circulated through the veins of black freedom fighters in slavery and throughout the black experience, in salvation history, and is also present in the biblical proclamation of justice, radical love, and human freedom.

Postcolonial theologies and critical reflections on race and empire are also important conversation partners in developing a contemporary understanding of black theology. One of the primary themes of postcolonial theory and postcolonial theologies that contributes most to the constructive task of black theology lies in its attentiveness to the past and present imperial contexts and its prophetic demand for "counter-imperial Christian action."[32] Postcolonialism particularly helps to advance theologies of resistance and a prophetic consciousness by focusing on the nature of identity. Whereas the exclusionary, fragmenting, and polarizing character of the Western, colonial, binary linguistic system encouraged exclusive and oppressive practices, postcolonial theory illuminates the discursive space between "either/or" modes of reasoning. It calls into question the very epistemologies and presuppositions that lead to the categorization and assumed polemics of organizing principles. In short, "Postcolonialism questions the basis on which 'insiders' and 'outsiders' are identified — the 'rules of recognition.'" Furthermore, postcolonialism, in its prophetic indictment of foundational elements of Western philosophical and theological discourse, "threatens the practices of exclusion and subordination that are based on those distinctions."[33] Postcolonialism offers a more global perspective of the oppressive clutches of imperialism from the perspective of the colonized — past and present.

---

32. Catherine Keller, Michael Nausner, and Mayra Rivera, eds., *Postcolonial Theologies: Divinity and Empire* (St. Louis: Chalice, 2004), 10.

33. Keller, Nausner, and Rivera, *Postcolonial Theologies*, 13.

However, translating postcolonialism into the North American context is a much more challenging task because of the culpability of American Christians in supporting and affirming the nation's colonizing and imperial explorations.[34] Since the mythologizing of European history associated with the Columbus legend and delusions of "manifest destiny," according to Barbara Rush, the narrative of American imperialism, in particular, with assumptions of "exceptionalism," "uniqueness," and "exclusivity," blossomed as a globalizing force through the growth of capitalism, Enlightenment ideas, the weakening of Western imperialism, and slave labor.[35] What postcolonialism does uncover are the ways in which religion (in general, and Christianity in particular) functions as a political instrument of empire. It exposes the often illusory relationship between theology and politics.

I agree with Joerg Rieger, who points out that "the problem here is not primarily with the relation of politics and religion but with what kind of politics is supported by religion, and whether the politics of the Christian God supports the politics of empire."[36] The problem of theology, and even the church, being co-opted by empire has been present throughout history. It has often represented the deep and persistent struggle for the church to be faithful in the face of incredible social and political injustices, such as apartheid and segregation. Michael Hardt and Antonio Negri, in *Empire,* observe that "in contrast to imperialism, Empire establishes no territorial center of power and does not rely on fixed boundaries or barriers. It is a *decentered* and *deterritorializing* apparatus of rule that progressively incorporates the entire global realm within its open, expanding frontiers."[37] Kwok Pui-lan also provides an insightful perspective of what empire looks like today: "With the decline of colonial regimes since World War II and the increasingly global reach of the neo-liberal market economy, the nation-state is not as significant as before. The new Empire is defined more by economic power, secured

34. See, in particular, Mark Lewis Taylor's "Spirit and Liberation: Achieving Postcolonial Theology in the United States," in *Postcolonial Theologies.*

35. Barbara Rush, *Imperialism and Postcolonialism* (Edinburgh: Pearson Education Limited, 2006). See also Michael Hardt and Antonio Negri, *Empire* (Cambridge: Harvard University Press, 2000).

36. Kwok Pui-lan, Don H. Compier, and Joerg Rieger, *Empire and the Christian Tradition: New Readings of Classical Theologians* (Minneapolis: Fortress, 2007), 10.

37. Hardt and Negri, *Empire,* xii. See also Kwok Pui-lan's "Theology and Social Theory," in *Empire and the Christian Tradition,* 23.

and bolstered by military might; war becomes a continuation of politics by other means."[38]

As I maintain throughout this book, black religion represents a particular engagement with empire, and prophetic rage provides a way of not only understanding that engagement but also opening vistas of wisdom to overcome a rampant culture of violence and nihilism in America and globally. The legacy of Martin Luther King Jr. in particular speaks to the essence of prophetic rage as radical love in action. In *Where Do We Go from Here: Chaos or Community?* King recognized the shifting landscapes of global economic and political configurations, and saw, through the gaze of liberationist movements around the world, the unraveling of modernity and its systems of hegemonic control and authority. In the last chapter of this text, entitled "The World House," King eloquently explicated the interrelatedness and interdependency of new global realities being made possible through advances in technology, global trade, intercontinental travel, and global communication systems. He also observed piercing parallels between the Roman Empire and American imperialism, proclaiming that America would share the same fate as Rome if it did not undergo radical transformational changes on behalf of the nation's poor. He pointed to Edward Gibbon's *Decline and Fall of the Roman Empire* as a detailed and intimate journey through the nuances, challenges, and fragility of empire.[39]

The United States and South Africa, with intrinsic claims of manifest destiny, modernization, and capitalistic desire, have embodied imperial visions of the world — with apartheid and Jim Crow in their shadows. What is compelling about the thought and witness of King is that they offer a way of understanding the languages of peace as alternatives to empire. His vision of community expresses the assertion that ultimately the language of peace and the practice of peace are part of the same reality. King's leadership in the movement challenged certain modern theological and philosophical assumptions about human nature and its implications on social and political structures throughout society. He challenged the binary linguistic systems (an either/or way of thinking rooted in Aristotelian and Platonic logic) that often lead to rigid distinctions and categorizations of which the system of segregation was constructed and sustained.

The violence of Jim Crow segregation — like apartheid in South Af-

---

38. Pui-lan, "Theology and Social Theory," 23.

39. Edward Gibbon, *The Decline and Fall of the Roman Empire* (New York: Modern Library, 2003).

rica, a racialized system of social ordering — was harmful on multiple levels. Violence was not only used as a means of sustaining and maintaining social control, but it was also celebrated as a nationalistic idol for identity and meaning. The world of segregation made little sense without violence. In fact, violence gave these realities meaning. Both the threat and practice of violence were religious forces of themselves that permeated the very air of southern culture.

Whether in the form of lynching and rape; the denial of resources in education, medical care, and public transportation; or white supremacist ideologies, violence was fierce and insatiable. The idea of establishing separate social systems built on violence reinforced modern theological and philosophical conceptions of what it means to be human. The most violent dimensions of these systems were, indeed, not just the physical violence, but the psychological violence that made blacks in the South and South Africa question their dignity and personhood as God's creation. It reinforced certain pervasive messages about black life. The denial of black subjectivity or the negation of blackness in modernity felt throughout the African diaspora provides a perspective of modernity from below. The radical affirmations of subjectivity and protest during the civil rights movement and resistance against the apartheid regime were embodied critiques of the linguistic, cultural, and philosophical forces of modernity, inasmuch as modernity had characterized human life based on a particular display of rational capacities.

Conclusion: Toward the "Postcolonial God"

The postcolonial God of liberation must be a God concerned with compassion and human suffering, which privileges the cries and stories of the dispossessed over against reason and personal autonomy. The postcolonial God is a God that places all human beings on equal footing, which creates the conditions for dialogue to occur among diverse individuals, and challenges elitism and hierarchical systems of power. The postcolonial God stands with the oppressed and those prophetic voices for truth and justice. The postcolonial God calls into question modern presuppositions and the systems and institutions they promulgate. In short, the postcolonial God must be a God that is looked upon, by the enslaved, to be a "rock in a weary land," a "shelter in a time of storm," and a "bridge over troubled waters." The postcolonial God is a God of liberation and the hope that fuels the task of liberation in the hearts and minds of the oppressed. As a black theologian rooted in the prophetic power of the black experience in America and throughout the diaspora, I am concerned with both empowering and liberating black folks, and offering up a public vision of liberation that supports the flourishing of all God's children, regardless of race, creed, color, gender, religion, or ethnicity. In this sense, as a black theologian and postcolonial theologian of liberation, I celebrate the shared destiny and plight as forever bound together.

The postcolonial God of liberation and hope was at work in the life of a young Baptist preacher from Atlanta, Georgia. When Martin Luther King Jr. mounted the pulpit of Holt Street Baptist Church, claiming leadership of the Montgomery Improvement Association on December 5, 1955, though reluctantly, he was not only leading an assault on the nearly 100-year-old system of segregation; he, along with other freedom fighters, was also challenging the very foundations of modernity and the underside of American history and her dreams. King, along with other critics of modernity such as Michel Foucault, Henry David Thoreau, Frederick Douglass, Sojourner Truth, Martin Delaney, Henry Highland Garnet, Dorothy Day, Mohandas K. Gandhi, Mother Teresa, and the like, brought into question, in dramatic ways, the cultural violence of racial, economic, and political exploitation. In their prophetic rage, in their righteous indignation and refusal to acquiesce in the face of tremendous human suffering, they point the way forward in an age that now stands at the brink of global annihilation and meaninglessness. Attending to the ways in which voices of prophetic protest, like King, offer a way forward to break the throes of nihilism and empire, sets the stage for lifting up a theology of justice and inclusivity in contrast to colonizing theologies of empire, violence, and domination, as we will see in the next chapter.

CHAPTER TWO

Empire and Black Suffering

Nobody knows the trouble I've seen
Nobody knows but Jesus
Nobody knows the trouble I've seen. Glory, Hallelujah.
Sometimes I'm up, sometimes I'm down, oh, yes Lord,
Sometimes I'm almost to the ground, oh yes, Lord.
Nobody knows the trouble I've seen
Nobody knows but Jesus
Anybody knows the trouble I've seen. Glory, Hallelujah.
If you got there before I do, oh yes, Lord,
Tell all my friends, I'm Coming too, oh yes, Lord.
Nobody knows the trouble I've seen
Nobody knows but Jesus
Nobody knows the trouble I've seen. Glory, Hallelujah.
Although you see me Goin' on so, oh yes,
I have my trials, here below. Oh yes, Lord.
Oh, nobody knows the trouble I've seen
Nobody knows but Jesus
Nobody knows the trouble I've seen.
Glory, Hallelujah. Oh, glory, Hallelujah.[1]

---

1. "Nobody Knows the Trouble I've Seen," Negro spiritual.

Empire and Black Suffering

> *There is at least one authority that we should never reject or despise — the authority of those who suffer.*[2]

It was a crisp autumn Saturday morning in September. We were preparing to journey to the Laundromat as we had on many other Saturdays. This day would be different. My father and mother had not been getting along. They were separated. He came to the house early that morning to talk, to try to work things out. My mother left quickly and sped off in the car. Moments later, my father left as well. A few minutes later, the neighbor called. We didn't have a phone in the house. Anxious as always, my youngest sister, who was only eleven years old at the time, rushed to the neighbor's house to answer the call. She ran back screaming at the top of her lungs, "Johnnie's dead! Johnnie's dead!" Our dear mother had been in a tragic car accident, killed instantly by an eighteen-wheel transfer truck on the main Highway 280, a road stretching across the state. I had never seen so deep a sorrow as a child sighing from the loss of a mother. Our country yard was broad yet overflowing with tears of grief as more and more people gathered. I cried like any child would cry, confused and bewildered.

My mother meticulously maintained a rosebush in the front yard, which now reminds me of the kind of quiet power Alice Walker spoke of in *In Search of Our Mothers' Gardens*. In her walk and graceful strength, she was truly a womanist in every sense of the word. Her rosebush was her space of self-expression, living out her own particular sense of beauty and hope in a world that was often overwhelmed with constant struggle and pain. For many years I looked on as she tended the small rose garden that was nestled in the front lawn. It was mature and well grown. I sat down by the rosebush and wept. Then, ebbing up like a groundswell, a thought rang out in my mind. I asked, "Why, Lord?," like Anthony Pinn in his deep and persistent probing of suffering in the human experience. As Douglas John Hall probed, I seemed to ponder, "How can one believe in God, a God who is at the same time good, loving, and powerful, in view of human suffering?"[3] By the rosebush, I held my first conversation with God, and it was brief.

The question, "Why, Lord?" that pulsated in my heart at the death of

---

2. Johann Baptist Metz, in Kenneth Surin, *Theology and the Problem of Evil* (Eugene, Oreg.: Wipf and Stock, 1986), x.

3. Douglas John Hall, *God and Human Suffering: An Exercise in the Theology of the Cross* (Minneapolis: Augsburg, 1986), 24.

my mother and returns again and again at the sight of great human pain and suffering, exposes the predicament of the postcolonial condition as it relates to suffering humanity across the world. As a student at Duke University Divinity School, I remember journeying to Mexico as part of a study seminar and mission trip sponsored by the Duke University Chapel. I was one of three other blacks among a predominately white group of twenty. From the moment we touched ground in the small border town of Nuevo Laredo, it was apparent that two worlds existed. We visited a very poor community on the outskirts of town. The people were curious at first glance and interacted directly with us. But in looking deeper, there was clearly a kind of resentment, indignation, and perhaps rage that existed among the communities. Their conditions were harsh and painful, even as they shared with us their very best. Our privilege was apparent as we freely expressed our wants, needs, and desires, tempered by the consumerism and privilege of Americanism. I saw similar dynamics and realities during my journeys to the shanties and slums of Cape Town and Johannesburg, the ghettos of Nairobi, and the crippling hunger and poverty of the Republic of Haiti. Their pain, in effect, like the pain of my mother's death, in a real sense bore witness to the violence of empire and its systems.

The violence of empire arrives as death, as tragedy and despair. The death of my mother swiftly and dramatically sensitized me to the realities of human suffering and pain. I would agree with Rowan Williams's scathing indictment of the whole history and breadth of the theological and philosophical enterprise in the face of Auschwitz, with the question of "so what?" The violent and dominating force of empire has never been more pronounced and intensified than in the lives of peoples of African descent in the modern world. So, perhaps a correct point of departure in establishing an alternative vision of empire would be to explore the ways that the black experience in its prophetic rage in the face of meaninglessness, hopelessness, and despair casts shadows of peace, justice, reconciliation, and hope.

Black theology, as a global movement steeped in the very emergence of global liberationist movements, has not, however, been able to adequately attend to the question of empire, and its multidimensional engagement in black life in America. Postmodernity, as a social and political condition, brings with it visions of imperial conquest. Empire, in its present configurations, is a child of modern thinking and idealism. Empire appears as the all-consuming beast of the state, exerting its political, theological, and economic interests all over the world. While America is not the only empire, it now stands as certainly the greatest on earth, amassing the largest, most dominant military machine ever known to humanity with economic tentacles expanding across the globe. So, for the vast majority of black folks today, empire is seen as the sheer magnitude of state power. It conjures up feelings of powerlessness — to change social systems, to fight against even local injustices because of their connections to powers and influences that seem so great. Casting a vision of hope and liberation for blacks in postmodern culture also means exposing the nature of suffering in poor black communities. It is often disguised behind the cloak of individual consumptive habits and the relative success of a massive anti–civil rights, anti–liberal government, antipoor campaign designed to position statecraft solely for the purpose of protecting and sustaining private property. I revisit the classical paradigms of theodicy in Augustine and Irenaeus, while demonstrating the ways in which stories, art, music, and literature also have something compelling to say about the inescapable reality of evil and suffering. The black experience with suffering in contemporary American life, in this chapter, serves as a case study for the canary in the coal mine, as an indication of much more pervasive problems that all Americans (of diverse backgrounds and socioeconomic perspectives) must take seriously. Here, I look to particular narratives of individuals and communities as resources for thinking about the power and efficacy of prophetic rage as a legitimate response to suffering and despair. I also enlist certain biblical themes of God in the prophetic tradition (Moses, Isaiah, Jeremiah, Micah, Esther, and Jesus) as a creative response to the nihilism and despair experienced by many in today's world.

The problem of evil, that persistent and inescapable question in Christian theology, has posed a particularly troubling issue to black life. For black people, historically and in present times, the problem of evil is not merely a theoretical one. The problem of evil, and the nihilism that it represents, has meant torture, enslavement, ghettoization, poverty, incarceration, and death. Theodicy, derived from the Greek words Θεός (God) and δίκη (justice), has come to define discourses on God and evil. The classical issue in theodicy, framed by David Hume, raises questions of God: "Is he willing to prevent evil, but not able? Then he is impotent. Is he able, but not willing? Then he is malevolent. Is he both able and willing? Whence then is evil."[4] According to Albert Camus in *The Rebel,* written in

---

4. Stephen T. Davis et al., *Encountering Evil: Live Options in Theodicy* (Atlanta: John Knox, 1973), 3. See also *Dialogues concerning Natural Religion* (New York: Social Sciences Publishers, 1948), 198.

1951, over seventy million human beings had been "uprooted, enslaved, or killed in the twentieth century alone."[5] The sheer magnitude of human suffering in the past century underscores the urgency of the question. Theodicy attempts to understand and explore the nature of that force or entity that is often marked by action or inaction. John K. Roth describes evil as that which exploits, wastes, and destroys the "sanctity" of human life.[6] It is viewed as a graphic and egregious denial of the dignity and worth of the human person. Howard Thurman, in *Jesus and the Disinherited*, suggests that for black people evil appears as one of the "persistent hounds of hell that dog the footsteps of the poor, the dispossessed, the disinherited."[7] It manifests as fear, deception, and hate. The genocide of Native American and South American indigenous bodies, colonization of Asians and Pacific Islanders, enslavement and murder of Africans, rape of women and subjugation of their bodies, and pillaging of lands around the world are a testament to the depth and doggedness of evil in the world.

Classical theists tend to follow either one of two streams of thought. The Augustinian "free-will" defense purports that evil enters into humanity as a result of human choice. Because human beings are endowed with the capacity to embrace or reject God, evil emerges as a human's rejection of God and God's way in the world. Originating with the fall of Adam, humanity's rejection of God's will is a continuum that creates the space for the persistence of evil. On the other hand, Irenaeus viewed evil behind the veil of "soul making" inasmuch as evil may serve the redemptive purpose of maturing humanity into the *imago Christi*, thus restoring humanity to its original yet mature state of being ready for final consummation in God's eternal kingdom. These two competing delineations paved the way for the modern distinction of moral evil (which speaks to human moral agency) and natural evil (referring to unexplainable events of the natural order). In either case, for oppressed peoples, the question is not whether evil exists or even the nature of evil itself, but what to do about it, and whether God cares.

In the face of untold evils, black people, as well as other marginalized bodies, ask whether God is both present in their sufferings and will come to their aid in resisting and conquering evil. Oppressed peoples do not expect God alone to conquer evil. They simply wish to be assured that God is

5. Davis, *Encountering Evil*, 7.
6. Davis, *Encountering Evil*, 7ff.
7. Howard Thurman, *Jesus and the Disinherited* (Boston: Beacon Press, 1976), 36.

rooting for them in the battle against evil and will arrive as a "coworker" in their march toward freedom, justice, and human dignity.

Emilie Townes offers a womanist approach to the problem of evil that links the quest to overcome evil to a journey of healing, wholeness, and liberation that goes beyond race, gender, ethnicity, class, cultures, and sexual orientation.

> The womanist dancing mind — the one that weaves in and out of Africa, the Caribbean, Brazil, the United States (South, North, East, and West); the Christian, the Jewish, the Muslim, the Candomble, the Santeria, the Vodun, the Native American, the caste of color, the sexuality, the sexual orientation, the socioeconomic class, the age, the body image, the environment, the pedagogies, the academy — has before it an enormous intracommunal task. One in which we are trying to understand the assortments of African American life. If I do this task well, I will realize the ways in which Black life is not my life alone, but a compendium of conscious and unconscious coalitions with others whose lives are not lived solely in the Black face of United States life.[8]

She goes further in observing that "a key way to understand the arithmetic of misery that evil invokes and provokes is to concentrate on particularities rather than universals."[9]

Recent events such as the Hurricane Katrina aftermath in 2005 and the shooting of Trayvon Martin, a young black teenager, by George Zimmerman, in 2012 also expose the multilayered nature of the violence of evil, empire, and domination. These events show how individuals and groups are caught in systems and matrixes of oppression that wreak havoc in our daily lives. Tragedies such as these cause one to profoundly question the nature of one's faith, one's understanding of God, and the way the world is ordered. There is a kind of meaninglessness to natural disasters. In a theological sense, it is deeply problematic to say that God was somehow an agent of such disasters. If so, what does it say about the justice and goodness of God, when innocence suffers, when children, babies, the elderly are crushed in the comforts of their own homes or places of work? There is a sense in which the meaninglessness of the awful tragedy of the

---

8. Emilie M. Townes, *Womanist Ethics and the Cultural Production of Evil* (New York: Palgrave Macmillan, 2006), 2.

9. Townes, *Womanist Ethics*, 2.

earthquake in Haiti reflects the ongoing suffering of black folks in America and throughout the African diaspora. An appraisal of the African American experience today is quite revealing. As the nation's unemployment rate teeters around 10-11 percent, the unemployment rate for blacks is nearly 34 percent, about the same as in many African countries. The U.S. Department of Education recently reported that high school dropout rates among black students nationwide were averaging 50 percent. So, one in every two black students is finishing high school, let alone college. As James Cone observed at this past American Academy of Religion meeting in Montreal, there are more black people in prison or jail today than at the height of the civil rights movement, when mass incarceration was common. Worldwide, the data is even more compelling. Prior to the earthquake, the average Haitian was living off of less than 20 cents a day. In most developing nations (primarily in Africa, Central and South America, and Asia), most people are living off of less than a dollar a day.

Prophetic Rage and Human Suffering

There is ample cause for outrage, prophetic rage. Prophetic rage is not simply an emotional or pathological response to meaninglessness and human suffering. It is not merely an intellectual response to the social, political, and philosophical problems of modern-day culture. It is a comprehensive, holistic (mind/body) perspective that draws on the collective wisdom, strength, resilience, and faith of the biblical prophetic tradition, the prophetic voices throughout history, and the narratives of enslaved Africans who faced down the dogs of meaninglessness and suffering through a militant determination to be free, human, and dignified agents of their own existence.

The biblical prophetic tradition stands as a testimony to the ways in which people of faith have, in times past, mustered up the creative resources to resist the tyranny of slavery, violence of the ancient world, and political oppression. They did so by first recognizing that God as creator comes to establish God's way of being in the world. God's way of being, the existence that God seeks to establish, is a reality that is just, good, free, and beautiful. In this tradition, they affirmed that God encounters human beings both as individual, autonomous persons and collectively as a people who exist in interconnected social groups (communities, societies, civilizations, states, even empires). Because this tradition was not beholden to the rigid, binary systems of thinking (of the Enlightenment), the questions raised and modes of social ordering have less to do with "who does what, when, how, and where" and more to do with what it means to live in a way that establishes God's way of being in the world. They understood that all areas of human life stood under the shadows of God's divine wisdom, justice, and concern.

It was this prophetic tradition that guided the history of martyrdom both in the church and outside it, in the great voices that have stood against systemic evils. Throughout history, courageous individuals have, in spite of their existential situations, resisted injustice. They did so necessarily without the awareness that full moral victory would occur in their lifetimes or that their personal or collective sacrifices would achieve their desired goals. They were able to engage in revolutionary acts recognizing that the process of resisting injustice, establishing God's peace and justice in the world, was a moral victory of itself. The process of speaking truth to power, lifting one's voice in opposition to what is wrong, in proclamation for what is right embodies a kind of generative, life-giving force that enables individuals and groups to thrive and flourish even amid incredible odds.

Albert Raboteau, in *Slave Religion: The Invisible Institution in the Antebellum South*, writes about the ways in which enslaved Africans (a deeply religious people in their own right) were able to construct sophisticated theological understandings of God as a counterrevolutionary practice for resistance and survival. Absalom Jones and Richard Allen, founders of the African Methodist Episcopal Church, Henry Highland Garnet, David Walker, Sojourner Truth, Phillis Wheatley, and Frederick Douglass captured the essence of the enslaved African's will to be free, to live with justice and human dignity even as the social and political context, intellectual structures, and theological teachings were all designed to perpetuate black dehumanization and subjugation.

Confrontations with Empire

To construct a theology of liberation for a postcolonial context, I would like to illuminate the ways in which King and Tutu, as voices of prophetic protest and rage, introduce visions of justice and reconciliation in the shadows of empire. The concept of empire, as it functions here, goes beyond geographic or territorial boundaries. The very idea of empire reflects a set of beliefs, ideas, rituals, practices, and symbols embodying its own religious system. Empire is reflected in institutions, structures, and systems such as the various branches of government, governmental agencies, state offices, and local municipalities. Empire also thrives within the ideas that inform and undergird these systems, like capitalism, democracy, and socialism. For instance, during the civil rights struggle in the American South, it was not simply that the system of segregation was legally sanctioned by the state and local government; it survived and was entrenched within the ideological culture of southern life, where black identity and black life were negated for the preservation of white supremacy and its privileges. The confrontation with empire, then, was not simply an all-out battle with the state (its police batons, angry dogs, and fire hoses); it was an ideological and theological contestation for the hearts and souls of the people. So, confrontation with empire and what it means for leveraging a postcolonial theology of liberation means challenging both the tangible manifestations of empire in social, political, and economic systems and those very ideas that give them credence and legitimacy.

How we walk and how we speak, then, become inseparably critical to the task of liberation in the postcolonial world. In this manner, language becomes particularly important for the task of liberation.

Language is essential to constructing new spaces of shared meaning, peaceful coexistence, and community. Language informs culture. Language provides the free exchange of ideas, narratives, beliefs, concepts, emotions, fears, hopes, and dreams. Language has a sort of timeless character. But language is not without its limitations. Language requires interpretation and functions within a particular social, historical, and cultural medium. The language or languages we use reflect the particularity of our own history, culture, experiences, social interactions, and geopolitical contexts. Too often, there is an assumed universality to the language used, which reinforces the reality of its limitations. As some critics of modernity have pointed out, there is indeed a "gap" between language and meaning — between the symbols we use to construct language (written or spoken, verbal or nonverbal) and the meaning we attach to those symbols. I would often hear it said in my hometown, Vidalia, a small rural farming town in southeast Georgia, "talk is cheap." We may very well have arrived at the moment in history that Richard Lischer calls "the end of words." The Duke homiletics professor says that in a time when so much suffering has been produced as a consequence of Christian language, perhaps preachers, theologians, and Christians should just "shut up." If silence is not an option, Lischer admits that if one must speak, one should do so with caution, fear, and trembling. So, there must be intervening factors that make the language we use, particularly around questions of peace, intelligible yet open to multiple interpretations and reinterpretations as new experiences and perspectives are brought to bear.

Prophetic speech becomes prophetic action, and conversely prophetic action becomes prophetic speech. It is a welding together of thought and praxis, what we say and what we do. In this sense, embodiment as a way of integrating a person's entire being into what it means to be human helps to challenge those Cartesian binaries and distinctions. We all know the famous Cartesian saying *Cogito, ergo sum* (I think, therefore I am) and *Dubito, ergo cogito, ergo sum* (I doubt, therefore I think, therefore I am). If being human means being a rational, morally conscious agent, as Cartesian and Kantian thought would have it, of those excluded from the range of rational capacities acceptable for entrance into the human family there is ample cause to not only enslave but also to continue to justify, even demand, demeaning treatment in order to perpetuate systems of injustice, fear, and violence.

Cornel West, in my opinion, has produced the best assessment of race and modernity to date in his essay "Genealogy of Race and Modernity" in his book *Prophesy Deliverance! An Afro-American Revolutionary Christianity*. In the essay, West traces the historical, cultural, and philosophical idea of race as an Enlightenment construct. He argues that the "binary linguistic system" of Western intellectual discourse (based on an either/or way of thinking) produced distinctions and categorizations (up/down, good/bad, right/wrong, justice/injustice, and black/white), where whiteness was equated with beauty and the good, and black as its negation. These distinctions ultimately translated into a vision of social ordering based on racial and ethnic distinctions, such as those seen in Jim Crow segregation, apartheid, and colonialism.

King, the Beloved Community, and Modernity

I find extraordinarily interesting the ways in which modern philosophy and theology have virtually ignored the voices of the prophetic. A figure such as Martin Luther King Jr. may have a monument erected for him in Washington, D.C., but in the fields of postmodern discourse, radical orthodoxy, or classical theology, he does not even receive a footnote in mainstream academic discourse. This is not by accident. One of the ways in which modern thought legitimates itself is seen in its detachment from radical praxis and protest. The postcolonial God, in turn, uncovers the myth of objectivity and critical thought as a legitimation of the status quo. In his prophetic age, confronting Jim Crow segregation, poverty, and militarism, King called these intellectual systems into question. He reminded people that human suffering, ultimately, is the final authority in understanding the nature of God and God's activity in the world. As Charles Marsh observes in *The Beloved Community: How Faith Shapes Social Justice, from the Civil Rights Movement to Today*, in his address at Holt Street, King situated himself within a historical and theological transformation that would have lasting implications in Montgomery and in the world. Marsh writes:

> The beautiful chaos that America would see daily on the streets of Montgomery — the tens of thousands of African Americans walking beneath a winter sky, the empty buses rolling through the capital city, the mass meetings overflowing the black churches — bear evidence of God's presence and promise. In the passages that evoke a host of powerful biblical images — the disinherited of the land, the long night of captivity, the glimmering promise of deliverance, each image as alive with meaning for the sufferings and hopes of African Americans as it had been for Israel in the long years of exile — King describes the moment as the beginning of a larger and complicated theological drama.[10]

King's interpretation of Gandhi's philosophy of nonviolence, Boston personalism, and the social gospel came as a result of longer, deeper, cultural conversations within the African American religious tradition as early as the eighteenth and nineteenth centuries in the quest for freedom. According to religious historian Lewis Baldwin, King was fundamentally shaped by his religious and cultural legacy. The Protestant liberalism of his studies was filtered through the lens of his African American evangelical roots and the prophetic preaching tradition that made it a divine mandate to speak truth to power. The Christianity of King's ancestry was a religion of resistance, of freedom, that speaks of justice and liberation. King was a

10. Charles Marsh, *The Beloved Community: How Faith Shapes Social Justice, from the Civil Rights Movement to Today* (New York: Perseus Book Group, 2005), 22-23.

product of the black church tradition and trained in elite Western educational institutions. His vision of the "beloved community" emerged out of his unique cultural and intellectual experience. For King, the black church provided the foundation and framework for his subsequent intellectual development. King recounted, "The church has always been a second home for me. As far back as I can remember I was in church every Sunday."[11] Lewis Baldwin's definitive account of King's cultural roots emphasizes the church's ongoing and profound impact upon his life and work.[12] According to Baldwin, the black church significantly informed King's personal and intellectual formation as much as, if not more than, his own family. King emerged from a long succession of black preachers. King was a fourth-generation black Baptist minister, so the idea of being deeply involved with the church was not unreasonable. King's father, known as "Daddy King," was well respected and quite active in the black community in Atlanta. Daddy King was also influential in civil rights in the city and through his involvement with the National Baptist Convention, USA.[13] Through this model of leadership, King was sensitized to the sting of southern racism and had unflagging responsibility to resist its unjust systems. Reflecting on his father's life in his autobiography, King stated, "With this heritage, it is not surprising that I also learned to abhor segregation, considering it both rationally inexplicable and morally unjustifiable."[14] King's cultural resources, to include his familial and church environments, are reservoirs out of which he drew his conception of community, for which he later established theological and philosophical justification.

King was well acquainted with the ways in which black religion envisioned an alternative reality that brought to bear a radical critique of

11. Martin Luther King Jr., "An Autobiography of Religious Development" (the King Papers, Mugar Memorial Library, Boston University, Boston, Mass., circa 1950), p. 8.

12. Lewis Baldwin, *There Is a Balm in Gilead: The Cultural Roots of Martin Luther King, Jr.* (Minneapolis: Fortress, 1991). See also King, "An Autobiography," 1-15; and Martin Luther King Jr., "The Early Days" (excerpts of a sermon delivered at Mt. Pisgah Missionary Baptist Church, Chicago, Ill., King Center Archives, August 27, 1967), 9-12.

13. Cf. Esther M. Smith, *A History of Ebenezer Baptist Church, Atlanta, Georgia* (Atlanta: Ebenezer Baptist Church, 1956), 3; Taylor Branch, *Parting the Waters: America in the King Years, 1954-63* (New York: Simon and Schuster, 1988), 30-40; Lerone Bennett Jr., *What Manner of Man: A Memorial Biography of Martin Luther King, Jr.* (New York: Pocket Books, 1968), 7; Lewis V. Baldwin, "Understanding Martin Luther King, Jr., within the Context of Southern Black Religious History," *Journal of Religious Studies* 13, no. 2 (Fall 1987): 8.

14. *The Autobiography of Martin Luther King, Jr.*, ed. Clayborne Carson (New York: Warner Books, 1998), 5.

America, questioning its moral claims and echoes of violence. As it was dispensed by the ancient Greek god of war, Mars, the violence of life in the South was both unprovoked and unpredictable. Violence in the South was an illustration of the ways in which violence functions in the larger imperial paradigm. It offers a glimpse into the complexities of violence as a religion, embodying its own rituals, practices, institutions, and deities. Max Stackhouse and Peter Paris assembled scholars from around the world to reflect on the nature of Christian witness in the age of globalization and ever expanding American imperialism and militarism in the world. In *God and Globalization: Religion and the Powers of the Common Life*, Donald Shriver Jr. raises the compelling question of whether, in the present, unfolding century, humans can contain their propensity for violence.[15] Given the fact that in the twentieth century, humanity witnessed the most horrendous acts of violence ever seen in human history (i.e., World Wars I and II, the bombing of Hiroshima and Nagasaki, the Holocaust, genocide in Rwanda, Darfur, Liberia, Sierra Leone, Bosnia/Herzegovina, etc.), human life is headed toward either sustainable peace or total annihilation. Tears of slain innocence still cry out in distress, restlessness, and warning about what could potentially lie ahead given the rapid escalation of militarism, nuclear technology, and cybertechnology.

The capacity to contain the potential for violence in the nuclear age may very well determine the answer to this question. Shriver raises another question that also deserves some treatment. That is, "can children of God use violence to kill some to protect other children of God?"[16] King inherited an understanding of Jesus as one whose ethical life points to radical self-sacrifice and social revolution. The life of Jesus is radical because it disturbs all forms of indifference to human suffering. It reveals a life, as Tutu describes, "for the other." The life of Jesus is a confrontation with empire because it poses an alternative vision built on peace, not simply for that which is achieved but for its path as well. John Dominic Crossan's analysis in *God and Empire: Jesus against Rome, Then and Now*, offers a unique perspective on how followers of Jesus, and those who have continued to fight for freedom, justice, and peace throughout history, pose a serious threat to empire, or in first-century Palestine, the *Pax Romana*, or

---

15. Donald W. Shriver Jr., "The Taming of Mars: Can Humans of the Twenty-First Century Contain Their Propensity for Violence?" in *God and Globalization: Religion and the Powers of the Common Life*, ed. Max L. Stackhouse with Peter Paris (Harrisburg, Pa.: Trinity, 2000).

16. Shriver, "The Taming of Mars," 151.

peace of Rome.[17] The noted historical Jesus scholar argues that the kind of peace promulgated by first-century Roman imperialism was "peace" achieved through military action. It was the kind of peace that requires an ever increasing and expanding form of dominance and violence for its maintenance and survival. In contrast to the *Pax Romana*, the "peace" of God in the world proclaimed throughout Palestine by Jesus was not simply problematic for the order of the outpost. It posed a serious indictment against the theological and political establishment of the Roman Empire. Whereas the world is constituted by the "normalcy of civilization's violence," Jesus made normative nonviolence both the means and the end of community and God's reign in the world. The kingdom Jesus sought to establish contradicted the political order and the way in which power, and ultimately God, was conceived. Roman imperial theology was built on the notion that power was characterized by strength over weakness, where might makes right.

> The first Christians therefore had to present a positive counter-mantra and a positive counter-program to Roman imperial theology's sequence of religion, war, victory, and peace. Victory, by the way, does not bring peace but only a lull — whether short or long — and after each lull the violence required for the next victory escalates. Is there any possible alternative to "first victory, then peace," or "peace through victory"? Yes, it is this, "religion, nonviolence, justice, peace" — or more succinctly, "first justice, then peace" or "peace through justice."[18]

Crossan's observations are not unlike those raised by other pacifists such as Ralph Waldo Emerson, Dorothy Day, Albert Camus, King, Daniel Berrigan, Jonathan Schell, and Thomas Merton. What remains constant is the idea that the quest for peace combines theory and praxis in a way that inevitably puts it on a collision course with empire. If empire requires violence for its very meaning and stability, then practices of peace and nonviolence in the quest for justice must be challenged on both rational and moral grounds. Empire and cultures of violence know what it means to respond to violent acts of aggression, but the unequivocal march of nonviolence is both politically and spiritually debilitating. Understandings of

17. John Dominic Crossan, *God and Empire: Jesus against Rome, Then and Now* (New York: HarperSanFrancisco, 2007).

18. Crossan, *God and Empire*, 29.

King's appropriation of Gandhi's philosophy often dismiss the fact that Gandhi employed nonviolence as a means to fight the British Empire. As Kathryn Tidrick observes in *Gandhi: A Political and Spiritual Life,* Gandhi employed nonviolent resistance to confront the systemic and ideological forces of colonialism and imperialism in India. King translated these ideas to the American South, but still recognized that his ultimate aim was not just defeating segregation but reordering American society toward a more peaceful, beloved community.

Although King did not use the language of empire explicitly, he saw the civil rights struggle as part of the unfolding of a cosmic drama of good triumphing over evil. Local demonstrations, such as the Selma march, were episodes of human beings working as colaborers with God to redeem human community, social systems, and a culture of violence. On March 25, 1965, King stood on the steps of the capitol building in Montgomery, Alabama, described as "the Cradle of the Confederacy," and comforted and inspired a beaten-down and wearied crowd of protestors who had marched from Selma's blood-drenched Edmund Pettus Bridge to the capital city. King said:

> Once more the method of nonviolent resistance was unsheathed from its scabbard and once again an entire community was mobilized to confront the adversary. And again the brutality of a dying order shrieks across the land. Yet, Selma, Alabama, became a shining moment in the conscience of man.
>
> There never was a moment in American history more honorable and more inspiring than the pilgrimage of clergymen and laymen of every race and faith pouring into Selma to face danger at the side of its embattled Negroes.
>
> Confrontation of good and evil compressed in the tiny community of Selma generated the massive power to turn the whole nation to a new course.[19]

He went on to say:

> Like an idea whose time has come, not even the marching of mighty armies can halt us. We are moving to the land of freedom. Let us there-

---

19. James M. Washington, ed., *A Testament of Hope: The Essential Writings and Speeches of Martin Luther King Jr.* (New York: HarperCollins, 1986), 228.

fore continue our triumph and march to the realization of the American dream.

Our aim must never be to defeat or humiliate the white man but to win his friendship and understanding. We must come to see that the end we seek is a society at peace with itself, a society that can live with its conscience.[20]

King's life and witness produced a global ethic of nonviolence, community, and justice, which characterizes peace as not just the absence of conflict but the presence of justice. He inspired a whirlwind of global consciousness across the world, particularly in South Africa among young activists like Steven Biko, Nelson Mandela, Allan Boesak, and Desmond Tutu.

Spirituality and Prophetic Protest: Desmond Tutu and Communitarian Spirituality

To understand fully how Tutu critiqued the social condition in South Africa both culturally and theologically, one must explore what Tutu means by community. Tutu's conception of community established the groundwork for his subsequent activities in opposition to the South African regime and informed his views on the question of the legitimacy of that regime. According to Michael Battle, the idea of community for Tutu cannot be divorced from his conception of spirituality that derived from his African and Christian origins.[21] Let's consider Tutu's social critique as a product of (a) his African cultural and religious views toward community and spirituality and (b) his understanding of Christian practices of liturgy and sacraments, as well as the social and political witness of particular members of the church in South Africa.

In terms of community and spirituality, Battle describes Tutu's conception of authority as rooted in the idea of an "African spirituality."[22] Battle contends that Tutu's African Christian spirituality is a spirituality of community — a framework that not only challenges Western practices of

---

20. Washington, *A Testament of Hope*, 229-30.

21. Michael Battle, *Reconciliation: The Ubuntu Theology of Desmond Tutu* (Cleveland: Pilgrim Press, 1997).

22. Battle, *Reconciliation*, 123-53.

ministry, but militates against it. For Tutu, political authority has meaning and authenticity in terms of what he describes as *"ubuntu* theology."[23] Tutu submits, "A self-sufficient human being is subhuman."[24] One becomes who one ought to be within the context of a community of others — both spiritually and ideologically. One's humanity is inextricably linked to the differences of others. Denise Ackerman, in her *Becoming Fully Human,* places this quest for identity (particularly African Christian identity) within the context of storytelling. Meaning, through the sharing and ascertaining of stories, solidifies social relations. Through the sharing of stories, one gains a better understanding of self, and subsequently a more profound understanding of neighbor.

Tutu's concept of *ubuntu* is similar to Paul Lehmann's *koinonia* ethic and the social ontology of the nineteenth-century political philosopher T. H. Green. Communitarian spirituality absorbs the *ubuntu* understanding that "a person is a person through other persons."[25] What many in the West and parts of the world under its influence (which could be most of the industrialized world) must see is the mutual dependency we find with

23. Desmond Tutu, "Some African Insights and the Old Testament," in *Relevant Theology for Africa: Report on a Consultation of the Missiological Institute at Lutheran Theological College* (Mapumulo, Natal, September 12-21, 1972), 42. See also Tutu, "Black and African Theologies: Soul-Mates or Antagonists?" in *Black Theology: A Documentary History, 1966-1979,* ed. G. Wilmore and J. Cone (New York: Orbis, 1981), 388-89; originally published in *Journal of Religious Thought* 32, no. 2 (1975); Tutu, *Crying in the Wilderness: The Struggle for Justice in South Africa* (Grand Rapids: Eerdmans, 1982); Tutu, *Hope and Suffering: Sermons and Speeches* (Grand Rapids: Eerdmans, 1984); Tutu, *The Rainbow People of God: The Making of a Peaceful Revolution,* ed. John Allen (New York: Doubleday, 1994).

24. Tutu, "Some African Insights," 35.

25. *Umuntu ngumuntu ngabantu,* literally translated, means "a person is a person through other persons." Battle contends that *"Ubuntu* is the plural form of the African word Bantu, coined by Wilhelm Bleek to identify a similar linguistic bond among African speakers. *Ubuntu* means 'humanity' and is related both to umuntu, which is the category of intelligent human force that includes spirits, the human dead, and the living, and to ntu, which is God's being as metadynamic (active rather than metaphysical)" (*Reconciliation,* 39). The phrase is derived from Tutu's tribal origins of the Xhosa people. *Ubuntu* is rooted in the Xhosa proverb, *ungamntu ngabanye abantu,* meaning "each individual's humanity is ideally expressed in relationship with others," or "a person depends on other people to be a person." See also D. A. Masolo, *African Philosophy in Search of Identity* (Bloomington: Indiana University Press, 1994), 87; V. Y. Mudimbe, "African Gnosis, Philosophy, and the Order of Knowledge: An Introduction," *African Studies Review* 28, no. 2 and 3 (June/September 1985); Mudimbe, *The Invention of Africa: Gnosis, Philosophy, and the Order of Knowledge* (Bloomington: Indiana University Press, 1988).

others in community. A person can develop some sense of who he or she is only in community with others. Through relationship with others, the concept of Christian identity is formed and molded. The notion of communitarian spirituality seems to develop through our identity as Christians in the body of Christ — a peculiar community of Christians. Here, the primary source of a communitarian Christian spirituality derives from Christ. Because Christ is the source of Christian identity, one's identity is only intelligible through Christ and finds expression in relation to others. This is best illustrated through the Lord's Supper.

Through the Eucharist, the concept of communitarian Christian spirituality is epitomized. Also, the concept of African Christian spirituality is commensurate with the Eucharist as being the intersection of community. For it is there that it comes together and moves the individual from self to community. The question in this context becomes not what I shall do for myself. The question now is, what shall I do for my neighbor in the holy community of Jesus Christ? Indeed, this way of thinking disturbs the very foundation of Western practices of ministry at its core by moving the emphasis from the individual to the community. Western practices have historically centered on a one-to-one relationship between God and humanity. What Western practices must ascertain is the significance of community and others in the worship experience. Indeed, it is within the context of community that we are able to understand how to worship and whom to worship.

The Anglican Church, for Tutu, provided the means for worship and consecration, which translated into his embrace of *ubuntu* theology. The miracle of the church, says Tutu, is that people of different backgrounds and experiences are welcomed with open arms.[26] The communion is the place where the interest of the individual is usurped by the interest of the community. One's thoughts and actions are taken away from oneself and placed in the context of mutual sharing and interdependence. Worship, the ultimate means for understanding political authority, reflects God's plan for human relations and the ordering of human moral life as well.

The awesome sin of apartheid, like slavery in the United States, or the Holocaust in Germany, was marked by a total and emphatic denial of the humanity and divine worth of the victimized peoples. "The evil of apartheid is perhaps not so much the untold misery and anguish it has caused its victims (great and traumatic as these must be), no, its pernicious

26. Battle, *Reconciliation*, 91.

nature, indeed its blasphemous character is revealed in its effect on God's children when it makes them doubt that they are God's children," Tutu exclaims.[27] Watered-down negotiations would only compromise the integrity of the gospel. This compromise would ultimately be a compromise of human worth and value in the sight of God.

For Tutu, spirituality and Christian practices reflected radical resistance to empire in the form of the South African apartheid system. By challenging those theologies of violence, domination, power, and control, black South Africans were able to face the battle against apartheid with grace, love, and peace. The injection of Christian practices declared a sharp contrast to the violence of the state and laid the foundation for the fall of apartheid in 1994. It is here that we see the essence of communitarian spirituality — a spirituality that takes into account the spirituality of others. Whereas the individual is influenced by the community, the community affects the individual. Tutu's *ubuntu* theology that emerged out of his African culture and Anglican theology recognized the importance of Christian personality within the context of church community.[28] With communitarian spirituality, there is a sense at which the individual is not free until all are free. Rooted in the South African context, this understanding is affirmed by Battle: "no one is a person in South Africa until blacks attain the freedom to express their God-given personhood and humanity."[29] "Communitarian" spirituality interlocks the spiritual well-being of the individual with that of the community. Hence, the community can never be what it ought to be unless the individual is what he/she ought to be and vice versa — "I am because we are."

Martin Luther King Jr. and Desmond Mpilo Tutu as Exemplars of Prophetic Rage

In the final analysis, a critical dialogue with King and Tutu provides enormous insights into the inner workings of empire and cultures of violence. These perspectives and communities lived out in courageous and prophetic ways alternative visions based on peace through justice and justice

27. Desmond Tutu, "Jesus Christ Life of the World" (keynote address for 48-Hour Women's Colloquium, June 17, 1982).
28. Battle, *Reconciliation*, 124.
29. Battle, *Reconciliation*, 124.

through peace. Both movements were marked by making connections — connections with ideas, narratives, theologies, beliefs, and relationships. Given the increasing realities of globalization and a more intense awareness of global and local fragmentation at multiple levels, there is an urgent need to forge a theology of difference that affirms the dignity of the "other" while pursuing a multidimensional concept of justice. Howard Winant argues in *The New Politics of Race: Globalism, Difference, Justice* that understanding how race functions in the global arena means thinking critically about the political, economic, religious, and cultural dimensions of racial politics throughout history. Race, says Winant, is above all political. Race and imperialism are close siblings in constructing and sustaining unbalanced power relations and the advancement of policies that benefit the few at the expense of the many. Throughout the nineteenth and the better half of the twentieth century, there was an unchallenged racial hierarchy situation in the Western world at the center of global privilege and power. With the rise of globalization and neocolonial practices, revisiting the concept of race and its relationship to empire would offer fresh insights to the conversation. Either way, the life and work of King and Tutu contribute to this debate because within their lives and thoughts are creative resources for thinking through issues of difference and justice.

One of the basic presuppositions behind King and Tutu's theology was that there were clear distinctions between the oppressed and the oppressor. Indeed, the system of Jim Crow segregation in the South and apartheid in South Africa made these distinctions painfully apparent. However, the problem of individual consumptive practices that are exploited by many multinational corporations and free market capitalism now complicates and blurs these lines. For instance, as Žižek indicated, through individual retirement accounts, mutual funds, investment accounts, or even shopping at the local market, individuals or groups may knowingly or unknowingly participate in their own oppression. As Douglas S. Massey and Nancy A. Denton argued in *American Apartheid*, often discriminatory and exploitative practices by large multinational corporations perpetuate cycles of poverty and exacerbate the ghettoization of the poor.[30] Consequently, it has led to a failure of public policy. Legislation like the Fair Housing Act (1968) and the Civil Rights Act (1964), and initiatives by the U.S. Department of Housing and Urban Development, though

---

30. Douglas S. Massey and Nancy A. Denton, *American Apartheid: Segregation and the Making of the Underclass* (Cambridge: Harvard University Press, 1993), 83ff.

important, have been unable to respond to the incessant reality of urban poverty.[31] William Julius Wilson has provided extensive evidence that within a postmodern context, economics plays a far greater role in the perpetuation of poverty among blacks than race does.[32] That does not mean race is not a factor. In fact, as Wilson argues, African American and Hispanic American communities still absorb the brunt of economic disparities. But the economic activities within the market forces now play a more significant role in sustaining and intensifying desperate conditions for the poor.

The interrelationship between globalization and economics has also heightened racial, ethnic, and religious conflicts. The fragmentation of theological and ideological differences, supported by the growth of global economic and technological systems, calls for a revision of liberation and reconciliation. King, in particular, forecasted this mounting concern when he observed: "All inhabitants of the globe are now neighbors. This worldwide neighborhood has been brought into being largely as a result of the modern scientific and technological revolutions. The world of today is vastly different from the world of just one hundred years ago."[33]

King recognized that because of immeasurable economic and technological advances, the ways in which the world was being ordered were forever changed. He observed the freedom movements sweeping across Latin America, Africa, and Asia. King acknowledged that the world was shifting its basic outlook by calling into question many of the fundamental presuppositions about human nature and social ordering coming from western Europe. As a response, he maintained that human survival "de-

---

31. Massey and Denton, *American Apartheid*, 186ff.

32. See William Julius Wilson, *The Declining Significance of Race: Blacks and Changing American Institutions*, 2nd ed. (Chicago: University of Chicago Press, 1978); *When Work Disappears: The World of the New Urban Poor* (New York: Vintage Books, 1996); *The Truly Disadvantaged: The Inner City, the Underclass, and Public Policy* (Chicago: University of Chicago Press, 1987). Wilson, as a sociologist, embraces many of the rationalistic presuppositions of modernity, and his findings are subject to limitless scrutiny and potential problematic variables, but his observations are nonetheless useful in understanding the complexities of the quest for liberation and justice in postmodernity. Although it may seem to contradict my earlier thesis that calls into question many of the assumptions regarding human rationality and individualism of modernity, Wilson's analysis supports an understanding of the poor that has been advanced in the work of liberation theologians like J. Deotis Roberts, Gustavo Gutiérrez, Jon Sobrino, José Miguez Bonino, and James Cone.

33. Martin Luther King Jr., *Where Do We Go from Here: Chaos or Community?* (Eugene, Oreg.: Wipf and Stock, 1963), 196.

pends on our ability to stay awake, to adjust to new ideas, to remain vigilant to face the challenge of change."[34] He passionately summarizes this view as follows:

> The large house in which we live demands that we transform this world-wide neighborhood into a world-wide brotherhood. Together we must learn to live as brothers or together we will be forced to perish as fools. . . . We must work passionately and indefatigably to bridge the gulf between our scientific progress and our moral progress. One of the great problems of mankind is that we suffer from a poverty of spirit which stands in glaring contrast to our scientific and technological abundance. The richer we have become materially, the poorer we have become morally and spiritually.[35]

King sets the precedent for an approach to liberation and reconciliation that begins with a serious reflection on the relationship between theology and difference. While keeping the welfare of the poor and economically disenfranchised clearly in view, King's perspective paves the way for thinking about the quest for liberation and reconciliation in postmodernity.

In his emphasis on Christian liturgical practices, Tutu also provides meaningful perspectives on approaches to justice and community in postmodernity. Tutu stands alongside figures such as Oscar Romero and John Howard Yoder who responded to the reality of human suffering and the quest for justice and community through the practice and celebration of Christian liturgy. Both recognized the Eucharist as the central intersection where the reality of human suffering and brokenness (personally and collectively) meet a God who redeems, heals, and transforms. Through liturgical practices such as the Eucharist, forgiveness, giving, and fellowship, human suffering is addressed and belief in God is made meaningful. Of course, Tutu would also continue this theme in the South African experience. Tutu's concept of *ubuntu* theology declares that persons are not ends of themselves. They are constituted through their relations with others. In other words, according to Tutu, we only become who we are through others. This view celebrates the difference of others. For Tutu, understanding who God is, and what God is doing in the world, is revealed in difference

34. King, *Where Do We Go?* 200.
35. King, *Where Do We Go?* 200.

and otherness. In particular, Tutu's work with the South African Truth and Reconciliation Commission (TRC) unveils how God is active in the painful process of forging community. Further, through community and reconciliation the activity and presence of God are brought into clear view. In the TRC, victimized persons were given the forum to share their stories of suffering and persecution. Forgiveness stands at the center of Tutu's ideas about community. In *No Future without Forgiveness,* Tutu argues that forgiveness is the window that makes reconciliation possible. God, for Tutu, is a God of both justice and forgiveness, in the Thomistic sense. As with Aquinas, Tutu believes justice and forgiveness are intrinsic to the nature of God. He rejects a utilitarian and humanistic understanding of justice that is not grounded in forgiveness and mercy. Because of the activity of God in Christ, the language of justice and forgiveness finds meaning.

His brief reflections in *God Has a Dream: A Vision of Hope for Our Time* relate the nature of God to the transfiguration of Jesus.[36] As God seeks to transform creation, the nature of God does not change. Love, justice, and grace become essential features that characterize who God is and the manner in which God expresses God's self in the world. Love, justice, and grace, as principal characteristics of God, are exhibited in community. Even the Trinitarian relationship between God the Father, Son, and Holy Spirit models the form of fellowship God intends for humanity. At the center of Tutu's conception of God is a communitarian ethos founded on a Trinitarian model. Tutu rejects the notion of an individualistic transcendent God that is detached from community and the other. According to Tutu, God is transcendent. God's incorruptible righteousness, truth, and justice are beyond creation. At the same time, God is not so aloof that God is not intimately connected with and sensitive to suffering humanity. Tutu challenges the modern assumptions about an individualistic God that seeks individual relationships. While God respects and honors our uniqueness as individuals, God views the ultimate good in the realm of community and social harmony. The following passage from Tutu is illustrative:

> According to *ubuntu,* it is not a great good to be successful through being aggressively competitive and successful at the expense of others. In the end, our purpose is social and communal harmony and well-being. *Ubuntu* does not say, "I think, therefore I am." It says rather: "I am hu-

36. Desmond Tutu, *God Has a Dream: A Vision of Hope for Our Time* (New York: Doubleday, 2004).

man because I belong. I participate. I share." Harmony, friendliness, community are great goods. Social harmony is for us the *summum bonum* — the greatest good. Anything that subverts, that undermines this sought-after good is to be avoided like the plague. Anger, resentment, lust for revenge, even success through aggressive competitiveness, are corrosive of this good.[37]

Tutu is a theologian of reconciliation, and Tutu's God is a God that seeks to alleviate human suffering, while also restoring fractured relationships. Tutu, like King, holds the belief that God celebrates freedom, justice, equality, and community. In fact, for Tutu the God who revealed God's self in Jesus Christ makes these terms intelligible to Christians and the wider social order. Tutu, along with King, consistently maintains that the gospel message is a gift from God, not merely for Christians, but for the entire world. The God who revealed God's self in Jesus Christ is the God who celebrates difference and calls the world into a community dominated by love and mutual understanding. In the process of reconciliation, God seeks to liberate and redeem social systems, economic and political institutions, and even history. Ultimately, Tutu's God is a God of liberating reconciliation, seeking to balance the theological dictum of community with the desire to overcome human suffering. Ultimately, the path toward liberation and reconciliation in a postmodern world must embrace the radicality of forgiveness and Christian praxis as rooted in Scripture. Forgiveness and mercy must be practiced alongside an understanding of justice that flows from a loving, caring, and merciful God — the God who revealed God's self in the ministry of the broken yet risen body of Jesus Christ.

There is also a need to establish a dialogue with King and Tutu and representatives of the United Nations and other nongovernmental organizations that offer international perspectives on peace. General Roméo Dallaire, the UN force commander during the Rwandan genocide, proclaimed to the international community on April 21, 1994, that he could stop the genocide with a mere 5,000 peacekeeping soldiers.[38] However, on the same day, the UN Security Council reduced his number from 2,548 to 270 soldiers, allowing the slaughter of over 800,000 men, women, and

---

37. Tutu, *God Has a Dream*, 27.

38. Jean Daudelin, "Rethinking Humanitarian Intervention," in *Building Sustainable Peace*, ed. Tom Keating and W. Andy Knight (Edmonton: University of Alberta Press, 2004), 1.

children within a three-month period. As Jean Daudelin illustrates, in recent years international indifference and irresponsibility have often "provided a shield behind which these kinds of abuses occur."[39] Several years later, the International Commission on Intervention and State Sovereignty (ICISS) emerged out of the UN Millennium Summit on September 7, 2000, as a way of assessing the "appropriate international reaction to massive violations of human rights and crimes against humanity."[40] The commission affirmed that the international community has the "responsibility to protect" innocents from unprovoked and inexplicable violence. In addition to international intervention, the role of nongovernmental organizations (NGOs) and intergovernmental organizations (IGOs), and international nongovernmental organizations (INGOs), cannot be overstated.[41] The politicization of these groups often stifles steps toward sustainable peace building. These groups often step in when people have been abandoned by the international community and at times their own governments. Leading groups include the International Committee of the Red Cross (ICRC), CARE, World Vision International, Oxfam, Médecins Sans Frontières (MSF), Save the Children Federation, Eurostep, CIDSE (Coopération Internationale pour le Développement et la Solidarité), and APDOVE (Association of Protestant Development Organizations in Europe).[42] To establish sustainable peace, says longtime policy expert Satya Brata Das, the international community must take huge risks and steps forward to strengthen the UN and to emphasize the global and communitarian decision-making processes involved in international intervention.

> Building a peace takes the international community into new areas: into violating the sovereignty of other nations, ignoring territorial integrity, and demanding the right to act aggressively against governments that violate the Universal Declaration of Human Rights. It is an implicit facet of human security — at least as advocated by Canada and several other middle powers — that the primacy of individual security must prevail in situations where civilians are caught up in inter-

39. Daudelin, "Rethinking Humanitarian Intervention," 1.

40. "Axworthy Launches International Commission on Intervention and State Sovereignty," News Release no. 233, September 14, 2000 (Ottawa: Department of Foreign Affairs and International Trade, 2000).

41. Francis Kofi Abiew and Tom Keating, "Defining a Role for Civil Society: Humanitarian NGOs and Peacebuilding Operations," in *Building Sustainable Peace,* 93-94.

42. Abiew and Keating, "Defining a Role," 95.

nal conflicts. The human security agenda in theory at least promises a future wherein human rights are paramount.[43]

Regardless of where one might arrive concerning the "rights" debate, the persistence and magnitude of human suffering demand revolutionary changes in international policy and efforts. When the lines are blurred and there is enough blame to go around between victim and wrongdoer, the challenge of ending conflict and forging peace can seem even more daunting. Peace is not just about refraining from harm, or intervening to stop conflict. It also involves confronting the memories, wounds, ongoing injustices, and social structures that provoke, and indeed cloak, the potential for violence to ignite once again. King's vision of the beloved community provides resources for the language of human dignity, justice, freedom, and nonviolence as interrelated dimensions of sustaining peace at all levels of human life.

Conclusion

Constructing a postcolonial theology of liberation and a black political theology for today's world must involve confronting the beast of imperialism at home and abroad on both theological and practical grounds. The witnesses of King and Tutu are examples of confrontations and triumphs over the compelling forces of empire in their respective historical and social contexts. The only way to effectively resist empire is through prophetic action, through the call to mobilization and resistance in multiple forms. Doing black theology in the present context requires engaging a multiplicity of ideas, methodologies, strategies, narratives, and experiences. The world has become much more expansive and multidimensional. As Leonardo Boff observed in *Global Civilization: Challenges to Society and Christianity,* theologies of liberation, more broadly, in today's world must be about making connections. In building on the prophetic and courageous protests of the 1960s, black theology expanded its dialogue partners to include friends across the globe in the quest for liberation and reconciliation. A confrontation, then, with empire means forming theological and cultural alliances with others who feel the stinging effects of America and

43. Satya Brata Das, "Sustainable Peace: Who Pays the Price?" in *Building Sustainable Peace,* 268.

Western global imperialism. In a real sense, black theology has always been about confronting empire. Even in the religion of slaves, we see the persistent determination of a people to claim their rightful place and be fully human in the world. They were hell-bent on proclaiming that in spite of the destructive and dehumanizing ideological and structural forces negating blackness, they could still sing with impressive volume: *"Every time I feel the Spirit moving in my heart, I will pray."* It was this sense of internal spiritual resiliency that allowed them to cast an imaginative vision of freedom and hope, undermining the very foundations of modern thinking and absurd imperial desires.

CHAPTER THREE

Resistance, Rage, and Revolution

If we must die — let it not be like hogs
Hunted and penned in an inglorious spot,
While round us bark the mad and hungry dogs,
Making their mock at our accursed lot.
If we must die — oh, let us nobly die,
So that our precious blood may not be shed
In vain; then even the monsters we defy
Shall be constrained to honor us though dead!
Oh, Kinsmen! We must meet the common foe;
Though far outnumbered, let us show us brave,
And for their thousand blows deal one deathblow!
What though before us lies the open grave?
Like men we'll face the murderous, cowardly pack,
Pressed to the wall, dying, but fighting back![1]

One of the ancient strategies of empire, as a global system of domination, is dividing and conquering. The impulse toward compartmentalization and cataloging, born of the modern world, on the one hand creates the space for an ever expansive matrix of differences that allows the voiceless to be heard. It promotes differences and recognizes the multiplicity of per-

1. Claude McKay, "If We Must Die," in *Selected Poems by Claude McKay* (Garden City, N.Y.: Dover Publications, 1999).

spectives, stories, experiences, and bodies. It poses a resistance to homogeneity, to colonizing systems of "normativity." On the other hand, it creates real challenges to building communities of resistance, for oppressed peoples to stand together amid larger threats to human survival and flourishing. In this chapter I argue that responding to this problem means rethinking our epistemological assumptions that have historically tended to separate head from heart, and looking to certain feminist, womanist, and *mujerista* voices, in conversation with postcolonial thought, in order to shine light on the problem of fragmentation in the shadows of empire.

Black Liberation and Fragmentation

Challenging empire as a primary task of the black liberationist project in particular will not be easy, nor has it ever been. It requires mobilization and solidarity rooted in a theological, philosophical, and cultural paradigm that counteracts the kind of fragmentation of black identity that we see today. Several years ago I sat down with theologian Steve Ray at a restaurant in San Diego during the annual meeting of the American Academy of Religion. As we got into a discussion about the issue of fragmentation in today's world, he described it this way, "You see, Johnny, for most black folks, before they even encounter the world, they are experiencing fragmented lives. So what you have is a fragmented self encountering a fragmented world, which only intensifies the various dimensions of fragmentation. When folks wake up in the morning and walk out of the door, you have fragments meeting fragments, which make forming community all the more difficult."[2]

The fact remains that the problem of resistance and developing a black theology of liberation involves some dramatic and meaningful expression of solidarity, social cohesion, and community. The language of postmodern culture comes to the vast majority of black people as a frustrating attempt to forge community or confront what Robert Franklin calls the "crisis in the village."[3] Whereas once the language of blackness served as a radical and desperate call for racial identity, collective consciousness,

2. Steve Ray is professor of systematic theology at Garrett Seminary in Evanston, Illinois. He is also author of *Do No Harm: Social Sin and Christian Responsibility* (Minneapolis: Fortress, 2002). This may not be an accurate account of the conversation, but I tried to recount the discussion and what was actually said as best I could.

3. Robert M. Franklin, *Crisis in the Village: Restoring Hope in African American Communities* (Minneapolis: Fortress, 2007).

and determinism, it now serves as an inescapable reminder of a disjointed and often intolerant body of people yearning for clarity of vision and authentic community. I suggest in this chapter that the fragmentation experienced in meaningful attempts to mobilize and organize around social justice concerns is also at work among theological differences.

Here, I consider the prospects and limitations of current debates around difference, and its relation to the black experience. For instance, as someone of mixed ancestry, Barack Obama is an example of the changing dynamics of racial identity in the black community and larger culture. Traditional categories of blackness are insufficient to fully grasp the complexity of racial and cultural difference. I distinguish between the kind of difference expressed in figures like Jean-Luc Marion and Jacques Derrida, and the more fitting understanding of difference reflected in the works of thinkers like Aimé Césaire, Frantz Fanon, John Stuart Hall, Cornel West, and Emilie Townes. I wish to make clear along these lines that certain Eurocentric notions of difference are limited when it comes to the black experience. Considering the ways blacks in Africa, America, and throughout the Caribbean have discovered of surviving and navigating the treacherous waters of colonialism and racism yields constructive approaches to issues of fragmentation and difference not just for blacks, but perhaps for the larger society as well.

One of the salient themes here is the interrelated and multidimensional nature of suffering and marginality. In engaging feminist, womanist, and *mujerista* theological perspectives, I discuss the ways in which women's bodies have suffered the brunt of oppressive and domineering social, political, and economic systems. I draw on figures such as Emilie Townes, Katie Cannon, Kwok Pui-lan, Jacquelyn Grant, Maria Asasi-Diaz, Amy Plantinga Pauw, Rosemary Ruether, Letty Russell, Mary McClintock Fulkerson, and Sheila Briggs to attend to certain colonizing theologies that sustain systems of oppression and domination among marginalized bodies.

In a postcolonial context, injustice is a multidimensional and ever changing, fluctuating reality. Depending on time and space, in some sense we are all both oppressors and oppressed. On the other hand, when translated into social systems, buttressed by economic, legal, and political might, the veracity of suffering and injustice is magnified immensely. The experiences of women and their lives as "text" serve as a critical resource in considering the ways in which prophetic rage becomes a necessary response to meaninglessness and intense suffering, seen across the global world. Understanding and hearing the voices on the margins (in an ever expansive sense), including women, the poor, LGBTQ persons, and others, create the space for a liberating praxis that helps to overcome the threat of nihilism.

How Globalization Is Impacting Black Identity

As I have attempted to show, there seems to be evidence that black radicalism in America has its origins in religious imagining. There is significant continuity between the religious roots of black radicalism and the subsequent development of West's "Afro-American religious philosophy." It would appear that West's thought provides a unique perspective on dealing with the lingering effects of Western philosophical ideas toward the oppressed. By appropriating the black experience in confronting systematic forms of oppression, with its various expressions in early religious leaders, negritude, Pan-Africanism, and R. Wright's writings, we discover new ways of imagining responses that seek to dismantle and disrupt the "degradation of blackness." Although varied in their expressions, the black radical tradition in America is relentless in its refusal to accept the suffering of racial oppression. Although Wright stands alone to some extent, he is also engaged in "imagining" or conceptualizing responses that spoke directly to the black lived experience under oppression. West appears to take up the mantle of resistance to oppression by waging an assault on Western thought and providing a fresh alternative. In his conception of an Afro-American religious philosophy, West takes into account the multidimensional facets of the black experience. In doing so, he presents us with a new way of approaching the question of black radicalism in a postmodern context.

Epistemology and Theological Imagination

The rise of the information age and the emergence of cyberspace and digital technologies have opened up new vistas of understanding related to the task of theology, the disenchantment and suspicion of traditional regimes of knowledge with their implicit (hegemonic) qualities. Critical questions of what constitutes knowledge and ways of knowing influence all areas of our lives as scholars, teachers, theologians, activists, and servant leaders. How we teach, the methodologies that we employ, in fact the theological perspectives out of which we emerge, are in some way linked to our deeply held epistemological assumptions about the world and the ways in which human beings experience reality. It surfaces in the tenure process of what constitutes legitimate academic scholarship, or in assessing student assignments, or in publishing in the digital age with the rapid move of the industry toward electronic book readers. Of course, while some stand in utter defiance against the use of technology in any way, and affirm the medieval, monastic qualities of theology as an ancient and premodern invention, and cry, like the great satirical American comedian Robin Harris's fictional creation Bébé's Kids, "We don't die, we multiply," the fact remains that technology has become a dominant force in the modern world, and that seems to be ushering in a new global, more fluid consciousness that is expanding ways of knowing and being known in the world. It seems to be creating new spatial realities, testing the very limits of our conceptual tools of theological inquiry and epistemological imagination. I agree with Boff when he says, "We are entering a new phase of humankind, a new level of consciousness, and a new age for the planet Earth" that will shape the ways in which Christianity and other world religions seek to "maintain and communicate a common message to all human beings and give a meaning to the universe."[4] Some of the key questions he raises are quite insightful on the rise of what he calls a "new kind of consciousness of global proportions, a new kind of reasoning that embraces the complexities of reality and a new cosmology":

> What will happen to the two-thirds of human beings, sons and daughters of the Earth, that find themselves marginalized in this global era?

> What is the function of religions, particularly Christianity, in devising the very thing (i.e. technology, cyberspace, digital communication) that connects and re-connects all phenomena; and that, in the religious sphere, deciphers the Sacred and the Mystery that are proclaimed within this emerging reality and that can unite and centralize all human experience?

> What is the responsibility of each of us in bringing about deep changes that are synchronized with the wider picture of things?[5]

4. Leonardo Boff, *Global Civilization: Challenges to Society and Christianity*, trans. Alexandre Guilherme (London: Equinox, 2003), 5.
5. Boff, *Global Civilization*, 1.

In light of Boff's observations, I'm concerned with how we create the space, theologically, for "difference" in terms of the underlying presuppositions of our assumed epistemologies and the ways in which these assumptions are reinforced in systems and structures that inform our teaching, research, and praxis on multiple levels. Differences related to our epistemological presuppositions tend to impact the authorities and foundations that serve to legitimate or delegitimate bodies of knowledge, which are also profoundly reflected in institutional and systemic structures. They appear, of course, as "normative" processes and yet are infused with particular epistemological commitments that appear in our vast array of differences and commonalities. Differences concerning race, culture, gender, sexuality, geography, theology, and ethics often reflect competing or shared epistemological visions of the world. How can we continue to create space for the voiceless, the victim, and alienated bodies to be heard?

So, in some ways, assessing our theological understandings of epistemology or ways of knowing in relation to current social, political, and cultural realities (i.e., technology, globalization, pedagogy, systems of power and domination, ecology, and the enduring quest for justice and reconciliation) may create new opportunities for resisting empire and overcoming nihilism in our teaching, scholarship, public witness, and service in the world.

A postmodern and postcolonial critique of knowledge emerging from feminist and womanist perspectives, as well as *mujerista* theological approaches, demonstrates the need to go beyond certain classical, binary approaches to ways of knowing, and their relationship to rising secularity in the public square.

For instance, Maria Isasi-Diaz, in her creative and courageous attempt to give voice to Latino/Latina bodies, has expressed her frustration and the challenges she faces, and the visceral desire for meaning amid the reality and depth of human suffering that continue to persist in the world. She was also, in a real sense, offering a radical critique of modern presuppositions concerning "rationality" and "personal autonomy" that tends to inhabit the abstract world of concepts, ideas, terms, categories, and distinctions that seem to militate against creative connections with the narrative experiences (or embodied texts) of human life. She seems to be probing what it means to connect and be connected with the multiple dimensions of human life, expressed in various disciplines, methodologies, vocations, and perspectives that lead to more holistic understandings and practices of human flourishing.

What does it mean to think about epistemological questions in the age of cyberspace where technology now creates new ways of knowing and being known, prompting the decentralization of knowledge production in local and global spaces? It is a world in which anyone with access to a computer or cell phone has the capacity to inject his/her voice, theology, epistemology, or theories into the public square whether or not it is named as such. Thinking about epistemological questions today has spawned a series of debates on the "postmodern condition," which is of course infused with its own hegemonic, elitist, coded speech, yet continues to influence various dimensions of Christian discourse in many ways.[6] The term or concept of rational epistemology (or *episteme*, "knowledge") and *logos* ("word" or "study of") exposes its cultural particularity as a construct of the Western philosophical tradition, and the ways in which epistemological questions and language, with its interpretive character, are seared together. Here, it is important to acknowledge that although the concept is helpful, human beings since the dawn of time have engaged in a myriad of ways of knowing and understanding the world, from ancient times to the present. The reality of cyberspace, in many ways, brings to bear our global and cultural differences concerning ways of knowing, what constitutes meaningful social interaction, justice, etc. It seems to me that what's at stake here is how we hold in tension the need and desire for all voices to be heard (of which cyberspace and digital technology now seem to make possible) with the pursuit of a meta-story of justice, liberation, and human flourishing in creation.

In some ways, revisiting briefly certain elements of classical Greek epistemology, because of its impact in shaping modern and postmodern cultural realities, is insightful. Mi-Kyoung Lee's work *Epistemology after Protagoras: Responses to Relativism in Plato, Aristotle, and Democritus* is very helpful in sifting through understandings of theories of epistemology and how it impacts our current context in a global world. She asks whether Plato and Aristotle were "simply unaware (or dismissive) of skepticism as a serious challenge to their own more optimistic views of the possibility of acquiring knowledge."[7] She wishes to clarify and thicken understandings of the prominence of Protagoras's "relativist arguments," alongside Plato, Aristotle, and Democritus, in the emergence of classical Greek epistemol-

---

6. Myron B. Penner, *Christianity and the Postmodern Turn: Six Views* (Grand Rapids: Brazos, 2005).

7. Mi-Kyoung Lee, *Epistemology after Protagoras: Responses to Relativism in Plato, Aristotle, and Democritus* (New York: Oxford University Press, 2005), vii.

ogy, on which much of the Western theological and philosophical tradition hinges. Lee's central argument is that "skepticism was in the air — not in the form of a well-defined school of thought or position, but in the form of certain loosely related ideas and arguments" as expressed in Protagoras's book *Aletheia* (meaning "Truth").[8] Protagoras's epistemology asserts, as in the famous claim, that "Man is the measure of all things, of what is that it is, of what is not that it is not."[9] It assumes that all human beings can and do attain knowledge, that knowing is embedded in the very fabric of human nature; that all human beings have the capacity to discern truth from falsehood. As Lee acknowledges, it poses a deep "challenge to the concept of expert knowledge and understanding, for it implies that no one can ever be wrong about anything." Although challenged by Plato, Aristotle, and Democritus, on the one hand Protagoras's theory of knowledge opens the door for a kind of relativism that has contributed to notions of equality and human freedom, since no one group or individual can lay exclusive claim to the truth. That is the sort of challenge that cyberspace, as a new spatial reality, poses for the human condition. On the other hand, the kind of relativism assumed in the world of cyberspace (sensationalized in the media, blogs, chatrooms, etc.) poses a problem to any claims of ultimate truth or totalizing faith claims that lie at the heart of the Christian narrative. This is particularly compelling when we consider the impact of Enlightenment thinking on the relationship between epistemology and theology, which has almost exclusively assumed a kind of Cartesian logic as de facto. Lee's summary is quite illustrative when she says that cyberspace "poses a challenge to the idea that reason alone has privileged access to the truth, for it implies that, in virtue of the sensory faculties and ordinary capacity for judgment that we all possess, we are each of us equally sufficient 'measures' of what is true and what is false."[10]

Protagoras's contribution to the Sophist school of thought is immeasurable and still influences conversations around human rights and social ordering grounded in what he deemed the "natural law of self-preservation."[11] These debates continue into the present where "Meaning and significance are no longer standardly supplied by the past but are now to be attained by searching and consciously choosing between a va-

8. Lee, *Epistemology after Protagoras*, 1.

9. Lee, *Epistemology after Protagoras*, 2.

10. Lee, *Epistemology after Protagoras*, 2.

11. William S. Sahakian, *Outline-History of Philosophy* (New York: Barnes and Noble, 1968), 26-27.

riety of religions, narratives, rituals, etc. — as if at a religious supermarket."[12] Modern theology's turn to human experience emphasized sensory "stimulus, perception, observation, sensation, participation, interpretation, savoir-faire, savoir-vivre, practical knowledge, insight."[13] In some sense, I find the notion that each and every one of us has equal claim to the truth, where the voice of the "expert" is on equal footing with the voice of the voiceless, very appealing. The Internet, with its varying modes of interconnectivity (with Facebook, Twitter, Flickr, Myspace, YouTube, GodTube, etc.), creates the space where a multitude of voices and perspectives are incessantly and perpetually disseminated, expanding our spatial and conceptual imaginations.

Now, of course, I am not willing to concede that the Ku Klux Klan has equally legitimate claims on the truth as, say, the Southern Christian Leadership Conference (the organizing base of Martin Luther King and southern ministers during the civil rights movement). On the other hand, I am also not willing to concede that we as theologians, including Barth, Niebuhr, and Tillich, and myself, know more about the meaning and essence of faith than my mother who raised eight children in the backwoods and foothills of Georgia either. One of the reasons the destabilization of "metanarratives" (not just an incredulity as Lyotard claims, but a "death" of metanarratives in the public square) is prompting a turn toward the particularity of stories (with all their complexities) is that it gives voice to both the uniqueness of individual experiences (i.e., ways of knowing and experiencing reality) and the deeper yearning for connections and relationality (of which the Christian narratives attend).

In the present cultural context, with rising secularity, what does it mean to do theology in the public square — where the lines between sacred/secular, public/private, religious/nonreligious, etc., are blurred and are becoming much more fluid (to draw on Stuart Hall) than ever before? For instance, what is the relationship between the reality of secularization and one's epistemological imagination? The jury is still out on what the cultural trend of blending, mixing, connecting, and reconnecting a multitude of ideas and information means for how we conceptualize the doing of theology, teaching and engaging in prophetic witness in the world. The question

12. L. Boeve, "Theology and the Interruption of Experience," in *Religious Experience and Contemporary Theological Epistemology*, ed. L. Boeve, Y. De Maeseneer, and S. Van Den Bossche (Paris: Leuven University Press, 2005), 11.

13. Boeve, "Theology," 12.

today, in terms of epistemology, is not the accumulation or sharing of massive amounts of information, but how to make sense of the continuing barrage of unending seas of information and the great abyss of limitless, unending, self-perpetuating bodies of information and knowledge production. The modern preoccupation with categories, distinctions, compartments and descriptions, boundaries, and borders seems to be collapsing (unraveling) under the weight of a desire for sense-making and meaning. Emerging is a sort of cultural rejection of binary oppositions and corollary ways of thinking, even rationalism (in the Cartesian sense) that militates against a sense of connectivity in both ideas and praxis. After seven hundred years or more of privileging reason and the autonomous subject as the path toward truth, there is very little evidence that it has brought us any closer. "Rationalism" as a central function of Enlightenment thinking is now being called into question as never before. And for good reason. To borrow from Foucault, rationalism can at times appear irrational. What Hitler did in Germany to the Jews was a form of irrational rationality. What took place in the form of American slavery and genocide of the indigenous North American Indian population was a form of irrational rationality. What occurred in South Africa in the system of apartheid and the complicity of the Dutch Reformed Church and English-speaking churches was a form of irrational rationality. The processes leading to the growth of the modern prison-industrial complex, and perhaps even the outlandish immigration laws of Arizona, might be seen as a form of irrational rationality. So, in short, reason is not always reasonable.

This cultural suspicion of "reason" and totalizing narratives and systems of thought (including Christianity) has always been present, yet it seems to have accelerated in recent years around certain social and cultural shifts. With the decline of the industrial age, in which labor and family life were the primary modes of social interaction, and the rise of the information-based society, in which digital and technological communication have become the primary modes of social interaction, the task of theology is once again burdened with the dilemma of adapting and remaining faithful, even expanding our epistemological imaginations, during these times. Technology and the digital age have contributed to reshaping identity, religious formation, and conceptual realities. What are the promises and perils of social networking, theologically — from Myspace, Facebook, Twitter, Flickr, blogs, chatrooms, e-mail, texting, etc.? On the one hand, it seems to create the space for voices once alienated, pushed out, and marginalized from the hegemonic and dominating centers of power and knowledge production. On the other hand, it contributes to a fracturing of identity and meaning, accelerating the processes of secularization and the accompanying nihilistic impulse. In either case, the relationship between epistemology and secularism as a fulcrum of a technocratic age presents a particular challenge to the present and future task of theology.

How might the insights of feminist, womanist, and *mujerista* theological perspectives, with their emphases on wholeness, fluidity, relationality, justice, and claiming the voice of the marginalized and victim, come to our aid in thinking constructively about the theological problem of fragmentation and meaninglessness in the present context? I was raised in a culture of beautiful, wise, courageous, thoughtful, and creative women. I am the brother of seven sisters, and have numerous aunts and nieces and a large extended family that celebrates the lives and witnesses of women in constructing meaning in the world. Those profound insights seek a "holistic" theology of interrelatedness, challenge patriarchy and systems of domination (which of course are deeply related to theologies of empire and violence), and eradicate "dualism" like male domination/female submission, male = strong/female = weak, etc.; they conceptualize new and positive images of women; and they rethink doctrines (on God, Jesus Christ, the church, sin, etc.) developed under patriarchal systems (i.e., conceptions of God as Father, Lord, King, and Master). Many of our images of power, empire, and statecraft, even how we approach epistemological questions and the ways in which knowledge is either legitimate or delegitimated, arise from the assumed patriarchal constructs rooted in the historical development of the Christian narrative, still bearing upon normative theological practices today.

How do we expand our theological imaginations in ways that respond to the realities of empire and globalization (with technological change serving as the primary means of their growth and expansion)? Because the forces of empire and globalization impact all people in all places (or, as Allan Boesak observed, "empire is everywhere"), how do we invite the insights of the global community in our theological and epistemological reflections? As North American Christians in the belly of the beast of empire, who benefit from its dominating tentacles, can we fully trust ourselves in terms of faithfully discerning the wisdom of God in these times? What ways are we engaged with our friends in the global world? After the 2003 invasion of Iraq during the Bush administration, a poll was taken as to attitudes and opinions about the war. Nearly 80 percent of Christians in the world, according to this straw poll, were against the invasion. The numbers were almost exactly opposite for American Christians, who, of course, overwhelmingly supported the war in Iraq.

Resistance and Revolution: A Postcolonial Critique

Resistance and revolution, drawing on critiques of modern epistemologies, mean functioning in those discursive in-between spaces. They mean on the one hand challenging the categories, distinctions, and presuppositions of modernity, while holding such categories and concepts loosely in working toward liberation and transformation. Postcolonial theology has sought to do just that. Postcolonial theology is a helpful conversation partner because of its attentiveness to the problem of language, culture, power, and meaning. Postcolonial theory — related to postcolonial studies and postcolonialism — is a "transdisciplinary" engagement that suggests "post" means "beyond"; "an ethical intention and direction." Here, "Western imperialism is the frame of reference for the term 'postcolonial', which emerges in the struggles of the colonies of Europe for their independence."[14] It serves as both a deconstructive and a constructive critique of the hegemonic forces of globalizing capitalism and its relationship to concepts such as neocolonialism, imperialism, and neo-imperialism — broadly construed as conditions of "informal subjugation of a sovereign state to a superpower and/or to transnational corporate priorities." Postcolonial theory (and its counterparts in postcolonial studies and postcolonial theology) seeks to move beyond the embedded "Eurocentrism" and cultural forces of power and domination that are intertwined with primarily Western (particularly French and German high theory) theological and philosophical frameworks. It challenges its "lack of a theory of resistance; its failure to cultivate a transformative agenda due to its detached attitudes; its revalidation of the local and its celebration of differences, which are liable to lead to further alienation of subalterns toward grand-narratives, which fail to take into account liberation as an emancipatory metastory."[15]

Perhaps the central focus of postcolonial theory has to do with the notion of "identity." It challenges rigid compartmentalization and distinc-

14. For postcolonial critique of knowledge (epistemology) and practices of domination, cf. Catherine Keller, Michael Nausner, and Mayra Rivera, eds., *Postcolonial Theologies: Divinity and Empire* (St. Louis: Chalice, 2004).

15. R. S. Sugirtharajah, *Asian Biblical Hermeneutics and Postcolonialism* (Maryknoll, N.Y.: Orbis, 1998), 15; in *Postcolonial Theologies*, 9.

tions, based in binary oppositions; and the ways thought and productions of knowledge were organized in corollary logic — "civilized/primitive," "Christian/pagan," "native/alien," and also categories such as "same/other," "spirit/matter," "subject/object," "inside/outside," "pure/impure," "rational/ chaotic," and on and on. Theologies of liberation and postcolonial theory are concerned with the ways in which these categories and distinctions sustained certain hierarchical and oppressive practices, surfacing in institutional structures and practices and expanded through colonialism and now neocolonialism abroad.

Gayatri C. Spivak, in *A Critique of Postcolonial Reason: Toward a History of the Vanishing Present,* argues that postcolonial theory focuses its "critical glance not specifically at the putative identity of the two poles of a binary opposition, but at the hidden ethico-political agenda that drives the differentiation between the two."[16] It is concerned with the process upon which these distinctions and categories are created and the powerful hegemonic forces lying dormant in that very process. Hence it looks to those "between spaces" or borderlands concerning identity, ideas, concepts, categories, distinctions, beliefs, and theologies. Mark Lewis Taylor, Michelle A. Gonzalez, Sharon Betcher, Namsoon Kang, Michael Nausner, Stephen Moore, W. Anne Joh, Marion Grau, Catherine Keller, and others are merely some of the thinkers that are doing theology in the crevices or in-between spaces in their appropriation of postcolonial theory.

Conclusion

Prophetic rage is a call for both truth and unity. It means speaking truth to power and existing within the creative, in-between spaces of fluidity and change, where knowing and being known are never certain but always and ever transforming, expanding, and being renewed. It is a clarion cry for celebrating differences, with a fierce determination to hear the cries of the voiceless and the oppressed. It challenges those totalizing, grand narratives and the coded speech that are disassociated from the stories of suffering bodies, whether at the hands of racism, sexism, and homophobia, or violence, militarism, and poverty. It means creating systems and structures that welcome voices of difference.

16. Gayatri C. Spivak, *A Critique of Postcolonial Reason: Toward a History of the Vanishing Present* (Cambridge: Harvard University Press, 1999), 332.

CHAPTER FOUR

Profits versus Prophets

What will happen to the two-thirds of human beings, sons and daughters of the Earth, that find themselves marginalized in this global era? What is the function of religions, particularly Christianity, in devising the very thing that connects and re-connects all phenomena; and that, in the religious sphere, deciphers the Sacred and the Mystery that are proclaimed within this emerging reality and that can unite and centralize all human experience?[1]

Empires, indeed, those powers and principalities that support them, have always cringed at the voice of the prophet. The prophet speaks for God and with God, in the power and authority of God. The prophet does not, neither is he/she capable of, compromise. The prophet would rather face sure and sudden death than to negotiate the truth. The prophet, though politicized, is not political. It is the prophet that speaks truth to power, whispers in the ears of kings and sounds the trumpets before the masses. Perhaps the only force at work in the world that has the capacity to challenge empire is the spirit of the prophetic, that bold and terrifying courage to say what needs to be said, what must be said, for and with the powerless and voiceless of our world.

Today, the role of the prophet remains the same as it was during the

1. Leonardo Boff, *Global Civilization: Challenges to Society and to Christianity*, trans. Alexandre Guilherme (London: Equinox, 2003), 1.

days of the great ancient empires of Bible times. It is to proclaim God's way in the world — the way of peace, justice, forgiveness, reconciliation, and radical love. It also means translating the social, political, and economic challenges related to globalization, the ecological crisis, and the valuing of human life over increased profits to all areas of society.

Along these lines, very little has been said about the effects of globalization and empire on black life, from the gang-blazing streets of Southside Chicago to the shanties of Cape Town, South Africa. The *AGAPE Document* of Accra has attempted to broach the question of the problem of globalization and empire for Christian faithfulness in the world today. However, for black people worldwide, globalization, consumerism, and global capitalism pose unique challenges to survival, faith, and the church, and for the future.

Constructive theologies of hope and liberation must seek to recover the prophetic vision seen in the ancient Hebrew prophets and martyrs of the early church. An unapologetic commitment to speak truth to power and the prophetic tradition's call for concern for the poor and downtrodden, I argue, must move from the periphery to the center of black social, political, and religious life. In this chapter I also revisit classical conversations and ongoing contemporary debates about the mission of the church (i.e., whether the church should be concerned with the particularity of Christian practices and retreat from active political affairs or the liberationist approach of the church's direct involvement in transforming social, political, and economic systems).

Why Prophetic Rage Is the Only Way: Globalization, Empire, and Black Survival

Lani Guinier, former candidate for U.S. attorney general under the Clinton administration, once made the gripping announcement that the black experience in America (and globally) is sort of a canary in the coal mine for the larger human experience globally. Guinier's observations merely reflect the global crisis we now face as a human species. The black experience, under the weight of empire, bears witness to the death-dealing storm on the horizon for all unless there is a swift, unified response to dismantle the current order of things.

The economic problem posed by globalization implies a kind of distance, emotional and spatial, from immediate experiences, especially when it comes to the American context. I would agree with Dwight Hopkins in his interpretation of globalization as a positioning of the United States as the "sole superpower throughout the earth and in outer space programs." Thought of as a religious system, not simply economic or even political in orientation, globalization speaks to the religious drive toward monopolization of finance capitalist wealth where global wealth becomes concentrated in the vaults of a small group of elite families on a global scale. Hopkins speaks with strong sensitivities concerning the African American religious experience and history of pain and suffering in America. He illuminates the fact that the ravages of globalization are not limited to Asia, Africa, Latin America, and the Caribbean, but also touch ground on American soil in the industrial abandonment of inner cities and the stagnating displacement of many rural communities across the United States.

Christi van der Westhuizen describes globalization in neoliberal terms. Because globalization is directly tied to capitalism as a global system of economic exchange, it is liberal in the sense that it advocates a certain kind of capitalism. She observes: "[N]eoliberal globalization is the increasing interconnectedness between states, through the accelerated movement of goods, services, capital and, to a significantly lesser extent, labour across national borders, a process enabled by political decisions to deregulate capital and liberalise trade, and by related advances in technological capabilities. Therefore, these 'intensified processes of spatial interconnection' are associated with capitalist restructuring and 'deeply infused with the exercise of power.'"[2]

Westhuizen's assessment is very reflective of the *AGAPE Document*, published by the World Council of Churches in April 2005, in Geneva. Westhuizen argues that neoliberal globalization, as affixed to empire, urges a kind of laissez-faire form of capitalism, or what some describe as unbridled capitalism. It has to do with deregulation of capital exchanges among nation-states and flows of capital around the world. Like Westhuizen, the *AGAPE Document* acknowledges the ways in which neoliberal globalization has become the dominant ideology of global financial institutions. It is precisely because of these global financial institutions and the underlying

---

2. Christi van der Westhuizen, "Power and Insecurity: The Politics of Globalisation and Its Consequences," in *Globalisation: The Politics of Empire, Justice, and the Life of Faith,* ed. Allan Boesak and Len Hansen, Beyers Naudé Centre Series on Public Theology (Stellenbosch, South Africa: Stellenbosch University, 2009), 3.

ideology, held widely by the public and faith communities alike, that neo-liberalism continues to be the driving force of global inequities. The *AGAPE Document* offered perhaps the most scathing and prophetic critique of neoliberal globalization with this piercing assessment:

> In 2003, 7.7 million persons owned wealth worth US$ one million or more. The sum of their wealth reached US$ 28.9 trillion, or almost three times the United States national product that same year. In the meantime, 840 million people worldwide are undernourished and 1.5 billion — the majority of whom are women, children, and Indigenous Peoples — live on less than one dollar a day. The world's richest 20 percent account for 86 percent of global consumption of goods and services. The annual income of the richest 1% is equal to that of the poorest 57%, and at least 24,000 people die each day from poverty and malnutrition. Environmental problems — global warming, depletion of natural resources, and loss of biodiversity — loom ever larger.
> . . . Wars rage in many parts of the world, and militarization and violence have become more frequent and intense. Joblessness is becoming pervasive, threatening the people's livelihoods. In a word: human life and the earth are under grave threat.[3]

The *AGAPE Document* serves as an alternative vision of global economics, one steeped in faith, justice, and human flourishing for all.[4] The document proclaims in very clear terms that neoliberalism reduces people and the earth as a whole to commodities that can be bought and sold on the open market. Neoliberalism or neoliberal capitalism offers an "ideological cloak for an economic globalization project that expands power and domination through an interlocking web of international institutions, national policies, corporate and investor practices and individual behavior."[5] Under the guise of so-called theoretical social, political, and economic analysis, neoliberal capitalism and neoliberal globalization claims

3. *AGAPE Document*, published by the World Council of Churches, April 2005, Geneva, Switzerland.
4. Diane Kessler, ed., *Together on the Way: Official Report of the Eighth Assembly of the World Council of Churches* (Geneva: WCC, 1999), 258. See also Richard Dickinson, *Economic Globalization: Deepening Challenge for Christians* (Geneva: WCC, 1998), and Jacques Baudot, ed., *Building a World Community: Globalization and the Common Good* (Copenhagen: Royal Danish Ministry of Foreign Affairs, 2000), 44f.
5. *AGAPE Document*, 9.

to be the best of all worlds, the most we can hope for under the present historical circumstances. It assumes that only those with economic resources are allowed to opt into the system of global trade; that competition is how exchanges are to take place; that labor and bodies can be traded on the open market; and that the free market (or laissez-faire capitalism) stands at the center. Neoliberalism celebrates deregulation of the markets and believes that private ownership of wealth, even in the hands of the few elites, is what ultimately creates and sustains job growth. At the center of its doctrine is the idea that markets and privatization operate more efficiently and responsibly than the state.

Global financial regulating organizations like the International Monetary Fund (IMF), the World Bank, and the World Trade Organization (WTO) were created to advance the mechanisms of free trade, on the backdrop of neoliberal capitalism. For instance, in 1985, under the Ronald Reagan administration, the WTO was established. Its primary task was to "enforce and expand the reach of free trade rules" in the global marketplace.[6] These institutions, the WTO in particular, have been strategically positioned to empower private industry and multinational corporations in order to control and manage global trade, transportation, technology, communication, energy, the production of knowledge (through intellectual property regulations), and human resources.[7] The rules governing these organizations are determined by the most powerful countries, which often set the conditions under which more vulnerable nations of the South are controlled.

Leonardo Boff, one of the founders of Latin American liberation theology, speaking from the perspective of the developing world, surmised that globalization is taking place in three ways: in technological transformation, in the marketplace, and in the rise of a new "global conscience."[8] What the WTO, IMF, World Bank, as well as the *AGAPE Document* and related responses to globalization such as the Accra Confession of the World Alliance of Reformed Churches have not emphasized are the ways in which globalization is also taking place in terms of revolutionary technological changes and an emerging fluid, global consciousness that they create. According to Boff, these technological changes, in particular, brought into being through social networking, cyberspace, digital media, and other forms of mass communication, have reduced human life to spectatorship

6. *AGAPE Document,* 19.
7. *AGAPE Document,* 20.
8. Boff, *Global Civilization,* 5.

and voyeurism.[9] Throughout human history, human beings participated in society through active engagement in consumption and means of production, as well as social interaction. Now, with the abundance of technological and digital pulsations, most of what we experience arrives to us vis-à-vis some kind of image or technological device. All reality, says Boff, has "become a mass media image" designed to program human life to be agents of consumption.[10] Social, political, and economic life is experienced chiefly through some form of digital communication, which removes the overall sense of human agency.

Experiencing all dimensions of human life primarily through technological communication is what gives way to a new emerging global consciousness as a process of connecting and reconnecting, navigating a treacherous sea of knowledge, in search of wisdom and meaning. I agree with Boff's assessment that globalization, with the thrust of mass communication and technological advances, is ushering in a new global consciousness. At present, the prevailing neoliberal globalization assumes free market capitalism and consumerism as definitive features of this new global consciousness. Whereas Boff argues that this new global consciousness, while currently being led by neoliberalism, is still in the process of becoming and may yet give rise to a redemptive, transformative, and just global economic system, only through prophetic action can the system of global economics be put to the service of all humanity, rich and poor. Only by recognizing that the whole globe, rich and poor, first world and developing nations, shares a common destiny will an economic system that affirms the dignity and worth of all human life be created that will determine the outcome of this new emerging global consciousness. Ultimately, economics must be committed to the flourishing of human life and the earth.

The Prophetic Call for Just Economics

While the current system of economics privileges profits over human life, what is the role of the prophetic heritage of the Christian narrative in help-

9. Boff, *Global Civilization*, 10. See also José Comblin, the Brazilian liberation theologian, "Sinais dos tempos no final do seculo XX," in *Varios, Vida, Clamor e Esperanca* (São Paulo: Loyola, 1992), 31-41; *Les chemins vers une societe de pleine activite et non plus de plein employ* (Seville, September 17-18, 1992), 9; Vide H. Bartoli, "L'economie multidimensionelle," *Economica* (1992); R. Passet, *L'economie et le vivant* (Payot, 1979).

10. Boff, *Global Civilization*, 10-11.

ing cast a new economic vision steeped in love, justice, human dignity, solidarity, and reconciliation? Recent declarations like the World Council of Churches' *Alternative Globalization Addressing Peoples and Earth (AGAPE) Document,* the World Alliance of Reformed Churches' Accra Confession, and statements from the Lutheran World Federation and from ecumenical gatherings around the world express the growing movement of voices crying out for change and revolution.[11] This symphony of voices is calling for a prophetic alternative to the kind of destructive and dehumanizing form of neoliberal globalization that now leaves millions dead and destitute. The present crisis of neoliberal globalization and capitalism demands that the common good become the telos of any global economics. In *No Rising Tide: Theology, Economics, and the Future,* Joerg Rieger says the only way to measure the justice and equity of the current system is through the lens of the most vulnerable and weakest in society. The common good is best measured and critiqued from the vantage point of the bottom. For it is from the perspective of those at the bottom — economically, politically, and socially — that the problems and challenges of the system are exposed.[12]

The *AGAPE Document* calls for an economy of life in which the following are true:

The bounty of the gracious economy of God *(oikonomia tou theou)* offers and sustains abundance for all.

God's gracious economy requires that we manage the abundance of life in a just, participatory, and sustainable manner.

The economy of God is an economy of life that promotes sharing, globalized solidarity, the dignity of persons, and love and care for the integrity of creation.

11. *Alternative Globalization Addressing Peoples and Earth (AGAPE) Document* (World Council of Churches, April 2005); The Accra Confession: Covenanting for Justice in the Economy and the Earth (adopted by the World Alliance of Reformed Churches, 24th General Council, in Accra, Ghana, 2004). See also the proceedings from the World Council of Churches Assembly in Harare in 1998; the WCC's policy on economic globalization from January 2001; the ecumenical team at the United Nations World Summit for Social Development in Copenhagen and Geneva, 2000; and the global conference on economic globalization on the Island of Hope, Fiji, August 12-16, 2001.

12. Joerg Rieger, *No Rising Tide: Theology, Economics, and the Future* (Minneapolis: Fortress, 2009), 156ff. See also Rieger's *Remember the Poor: The Challenge to Theology in the Twenty-First Century* (Harrisburg, Pa.: Trinity, 1998), and Ulrich Duchrow and Franz J. Hinkelammert's *Property for People, Not for Profit: Alternatives to the Global Tyranny of Capital* (New York: Zed Books, 2004).

God's economy is an economy for the whole *oikoumene* — the whole
earth community.
God's justice and preferential option for the poor are the marks of
God's economy.[13]

The need for a new global vision for economics that is driven by human flourishing and not the accumulation of profits is reflected in all dimensions of society. It is perhaps most felt in the ghettos, shanties, slums,
and depressed urban communities around the world. Since the groundbreaking work of William Julius Wilson in the book *The Declining Significance of Race,* critical social analysis of the urban poor has claimed serious
attention. Wilson makes clear that the economic disparities being generated
across the globe are deeply interwoven with the disappearance of work and
its consequences to social, economic, and cultural life in inner-city ghettos.

Ironically, the nation now remembers both the 400th anniversary of
the Jamestown settlement and the 40th anniversary of the Poor People's
Campaign, the final pilgrimage of hope envisioned in the prophetic leadership of Martin Luther King Jr. King saw on the horizon a radical decentralization of European power and the movement of power in the world to
America and the thrust of free market capitalism. The intensification of
technological advances and the promulgation of mass media and access to
travel, for King, meant that the world must begin to radically reorganize its
economic commitments concerning the poor. He introduced the concept
of a "bill of rights" for the poor as a step toward a democratic socialist vision of society, which he believed lay at the heart of the Judeo-Christian
faith. The challenge before us today is to contextualize King's vision as we
forge a progressive urban agenda for the African American community.
Which means, we must begin to affirm the reality that God is concerned
with all areas of human life, including the social, political, economic, and
cultural dimensions of our experience. Working toward just public policy
is as essential to worship of God as what occurs within the context of the
church on Sunday morning. The Holy Spirit, according to the Latin American theologian Gustavo Gutiérrez, is at work wherever the activity of justice, mercy, and human freedom abides.

In *Empire and the Christian Tradition* and Max Stackhouse's *God and*

13. *AGAPE Document,* 4. See also "Criteria towards Economic Policy-Making," in the
WCC study document "Christian Faith and the World Economy Today" (Geneva: WCC,
1992), 29.

Globalization, it becomes apparent that the issue of globalization is not just a social and economic crisis, but a complex theological and ethical dilemma as well. For instance, Kwok Pui-lan offers a compelling analysis concerning the shifting dynamics of "imperialism" and "empire" in the contemporary world. He also discusses the ways in which the Christian tradition has often found itself deeply "entangled" in the working out of these forces in public life. Pui-lan opens the door for addressing the critical question of why Christians, in general, and theologians in particular ought to be concerned about the language of "empire." He rightly begins the conversation with the relationship between theology and social theory. Since the rise of modernity during the Enlightenment period, a cultural trend of understanding political discourse as chiefly a social scientific project has posed considerable problems for theologians who recognize God's involvement with all areas of human life.

The rigid compartmentalization that, according to John Milbank, relegated theology and the church to the private sphere of the sublime is contrary to envisioning God as creator and sustainer of all life and reality, including governments and political and economic institutions. Pui-lan observes that earlier forms of imperialism were marked by military and political control of foreign territories, while the present notion of empire is dramatically different. It is much more expressed as "economic power, secured and bolstered by military might; war becomes a continuation of politics by other means."[14] Drawing on Michael Hardt and Antonio Negri's analysis in *Empire,* Pui-lan calls for an approach to understanding globalization from the perspective of those who do not have the capacity to participate in its promises, hopes, and dreams.

What is perhaps most challenging about the relationship between the Christian tradition and empire surrounds conceptions of God, and occurs in human affairs as human beings attempt to emulate and live out the divine image. If human beings conceptualize God as "power," "will," "sovereignty," and "dominion," then human beings (as created in the image of God) gain divine mandate in acquiring more power, dominance, control, and sovereignty in the world, and advancing empire along the way. So, Pui-lan, Compier, Wiley, Lyman, Chvala-Smith, Grau, McFarland, Ray, and Farley all attest to the ways in which Christian theology is deeply embedded in the historical, political, and economic unfolding of empire,

---

14. Kwok Pui-lan, Don H. Compier, and Joerg Rieger, eds., *Empire and the Christian Tradition: New Readings of Classical Theologians* (Minneapolis: Fortress, 2007), 23.

from Rome to the United States. For instance, if we consider Chvala-Smith's assessment of Augustine's critique of Roman imperialism in the *City of God,* Christians have reason to be suspicious of any attempts to assign divine sanction to any nation-state, political system, or economic system. According to Chvala-Smith, Augustine's distinction between the city of God and the earthly city offers a scathing critique of propping up a particular political system as having theological justification. The city of God always comes in its earthly pilgrimage to proclaim justice, peace, and mercy; it seeks to directly challenge and transform the present order in witness to God's glory and reign.

I wish Chvala-Smith had given more attention in his essay to the ways in which the church, throughout history and into the present, has often found itself a complicit actor in the work of empire. From the crowning of Christianity as the "official" state religion under Emperor Constantine in the fourth century to the christening of American democratization and neoliberalism abroad, it is imperative to reflect on the prophetic and imaginative narratives in the Christian tradition that sought to advance alternative communities of resistance, reconciliation, nonviolence, justice, and hope. Overall, the reading provides a compelling inroad into making connections between the contemporary challenges of understanding empire and globalization, and the historical unfolding of the Christian narrative. If it is correct in assessing the relationship between God and empire, how do we begin to reconceptualize who God is and what would be the implications for the church?

Faith in the Marketplace: A Theological Perspective on Christian Beliefs and Economics

There is a sense in which the history of economic exchanges mirrors the history of humanity's experience in community and religious belief. There is no time in history when human beings have not had to grapple with questions of economic exchanges of goods, services, even ideas (i.e., intellectual property) and bodies (slavery, indentured servitude, exploitation of labor). The Judeo-Christian faith, in many ways as part of the long history of the people of Israel, has mostly been preoccupied with the issue of fairness or equality in the marketplace and with expressing a deep concern for the poor and marginalized, essentially those left out of the whole process.

Economy, from the Greek term *oikonomos,* from the term *oikos* (house), used to describe household management, presupposing some sort of system designed to navigate human interactions for living and existing in community. In the book *Divine Economy: Theology and the Market,* Steve Long raises the question, "What has theology to do with the economy?" He says that "Given the standpoint of the average economics textbook, the answer from the economists' perspective is obvious: nothing. Theology might have relevance for the cultural values that undergird the economic system, but actual economic practice is best served when theology keeps its own proper sphere. Premodern theological efforts to speak a decisive word on economic practice are described by both economists and many theologians as misguided, irrational, and authoritarian."[15]

In spite of this assertion and public perception, many theologians, says Long, have stressed the "ancient tradition that faith and economic matters are inextricably linked."[16] God's economy, according to Long, establishes a dramatic critique of the ways in which the modern economic system, which assumes to operate out of its own metaphysical forces, has taken on a profound antihumane tone. God's economy comes to challenge forms of exploitation, unchecked consumerism, and economic practices that devalue life, communities, and the earth. Practices such as the Eucharist, forgiveness, Year of Jubilee, service, prayer, basin and towel are not simply theological categories with no relevance to the marketplace. Rather, they serve as tangible insights on what it means to engage in fruitful and meaningful economic exchanges and human social life. These practices apply to all areas of human life, including business affairs.

These sentiments were expressed, for instance, in the nineteenth-century debates on usury in Britain concerning the ethical problem of credit and charging interest on loans. Christian theology offers a prophetic critique against predatory lending practices and the exploitatively high concentration of liquor stores in impoverished communities, which leech the scarce economic resources of those communities without giving back to them. It mirrors apartheid structures where people live in places where they do not work and persons do business where they do not live.

15. D. Stephen Long, *Divine Economy: Theology and the Market* (New York: Routledge, 2000), 15.
16. Long, *Divine Economy,* 15.

Envisioning Business for the Common Good

How can we recover the significance of social responsibility in the market-place? Local business practices now have global significance. Globalization is rising and a dramatic shift is taking place from an industrialized economy to an information/technological economic system. Increases in technology have contributed to the rise of small business through networking and more efficient ways of engaging in economic exchanges. Organizations such as the International Monetary Fund, the World Bank, and the G8 (the world's eight largest economies) now direct the conditions for economic growth and expansion fueled by local business activities. Though global, they recognize that at the end of the day, all business is local.

Theologians are concerned because economics have a tremendous impact on the spiritual and material vitality of human beings and the earth. Embracing the reality that human beings are reflecting the divine image of God means that people of faith must be concerned and alarmed when mistreatment, abuse, neglect, or marginalization takes place. Perhaps for the first time in human history, human beings now have the capacity through technology to feed the entire world. But greed, over-consumerism, and the quest for power continue to pose serious challenges to this process.

Capitalism and the Crisis of the Prophetic in the Pulpit

The problematic dimensions of the prosperity gospel, as well as the profligate lifestyles of many well-to-do megachurch pastors, have received much attention due to the contrasting issues of poverty, gang violence, and homelessness in the black community. Jonathan Walton's book *Watch This!* identified several key figures in the historical development of the prosperity gospel and televangelism. Walton's critique was levied toward the materialism and sensationalism that have so accurately characterized African American leaders in many of the large-church pulpits around the nation. While Walton was indeed right to point out the problems of economic exploitation in the pulpit, Walton's inability to draw connections between the actions of black preachers who subscribe to the forces of capitalism and consumerism and the overarching structures of empire that fuel these activities reflects a misguided and misdirected concern.

The real problem is not just black preachers in the pulpits who proclaim the prosperity gospel or attempt to justify extravagant lifestyles of wealth and materialism. Perhaps the greater issue is at work in the empire that gives it life and is sustained and buttressed by theological, political, economic, and intellectual systems. It is not simply black televangelists or prosperity preachers who are caught up in the matrix of empire and capitalism. Mainline churches and denominations, universities and colleges, endowed churches and seminaries, mission societies, and other organizations boasting hedge funds and multimillion-dollar portfolios and pension funds all participate in a culture of consumerism and empire.

The forces of secularization have problematized the prophetic voice of the black church, often making the work of Martin Luther King Jr. and the freedom fighters of old offensive in today's sensationalistic pseudo-Pentecostal church. As Walton emphasizes, the megachurch phenomenon deserves specific attention because of its effect on the larger public. In a sense, it has become the heir apparent of empire, capitalism, and a culture driven by materialism and consumerism. It represents a fusion of the secularization of traditional religion and Pentecostalism/charismaticism/evangelicalism that connects local and global spaces. By emphasizing "relevance" and responding to the needs of the unchurched, megachurches have capitalized on the tools of marketing, corporate organizational management, and contemporary aesthetics in becoming multimillion-dollar operations. Their *theo-ideology* resonates well with the mainstream neoliberalism pervasive in the public square.

Ostwalt's book *Secular Steeples* provides insight into the ways in which Christianity, in particular, as part of an imperialistic and global economic giant, has also fallen prey to the allusive lure of capitalism.[17] That capitalistic impulse and desire have infused themselves into the Christian message through the illusion of self-empowerment, determinism, and individual consumption. In a few years we will celebrate the fiftieth anniversary of the Poor People's Campaign, introduced by Martin Luther King Jr. in 1967, with his call for a national bill of rights for the poor. On the backdrop of his historic speech before a crowded gathering of clergy at the Riverside Church in New York critiquing the Vietnam War, King recognized that there are no invisible forces that control the market. But often the market is ordered through politics and power to benefit the very wealthy few. Structures must then be put into place in local spaces, as well as na-

17. Conrad Ostwalt, *Secular Steeples: Popular Culture and the Religious Imagination* (Harrisburg, Pa.: Trinity, 2003).

tionally and internationally, to preserve the dignity of the poor, and to provide safeguards from the blind spots of capitalism, greed, and exploitation.

Gustavo Gutiérrez, Michael Novak, and the Problem of Competing Theological Visions

While black religion and black theology have confronted the economic and political problems faced by oppressed peoples historically and in today's time, the black experience does not stand alone in critiquing and understanding the nuances of theology and the marketplace. Gustavo Gutiérrez continues to stand as a towering figure in theological reflections on capitalism and empire, and the ways in which the battle that must be had among Christians in the Western world must be waged on theological grounds. On the other side of Gutiérrez stands Michael Novak, who sees the rising prominence of globalization, capitalism, and imperialism as a visible expression of the church's witness in the world. Exploring the dialogue between Gutiérrez and Novak is essential to providing a framework for the larger battle between prophets and profits today.

The declining significance of nation-states, due to the rise and influence of multinational corporations, presents new challenges on how to think about issues of "justice," economics, and "ecclesiology" in a postmodern era. The task here is to examine the question of human fulfillment and liberation in Novak and Gutiérrez with implications toward economics in a postmodern context. The fundamental distinction between Novak and Gutiérrez relates to how each thinker approaches and characterizes human fulfillment and liberation.

Novak seeks to describe the "corporation" (as an expression of the free market economy) in the language of Catholicism. He attempts to expand and reinterpret such theological categories as "grace," "spirit," and "solidarity." Novak aims to appropriate Christian language in order to advance the notion of a free market economy, unrestrained by state or private regulation. Gutiérrez, however, develops his argument by an appeal to the historical quest for "human fulfillment." The presence of God, for Gutiérrez, is revealed in the drumbeat of liberation. Hence, the market, if it is to have any legitimacy, must mediate the liberation process. As Steve Long points out, the critical distinction between Novak and Gutiérrez concerns how they view global economic marketing systems. Drawing from a Marxist critique, Gutiérrez posits that capitalism by its very nature is oppressive, because it relies heavily on the exploitation of labor in order to function. Novak, on the other hand, sees the market as an uninhibited reality that operates on the basis of utility, much in the same vein as Bentham and the school of utilitarianism.

Novak and Gutiérrez inherited presumed theories and practices concerning the market economy. Two important figures shaping modern assumptions about the market, particularly capitalism, were Adam Ferguson and Adam Smith. Both Edinburgh professors, they conceived of society in the form of a living human body made of many components, organs, and extremities. Believing society consisted of parts, Ferguson developed ideas around division of labor and systems of exchange for goods and services. Ferguson held that, like the body, divisions of labor are able to carry out necessary exchanges on their own. Smith expanded on these ideas in *The Wealth of Nations* (1776, bk. 1, chap. 8). Smith held that the market functioned by its own set of laws and procedures based on supply and demand. The principle of supply and demand, he argued, operated in a way that benefited all involved. Liberalism emerged, fusing economics and political philosophy together as scientific disciplines.

The Earth Is the Lord's!
Prophets, Profits, and the Ecological Crisis

I am constantly amazed by the repeated deletion, exclusion, dismissal, and denial of the voices of indigenous and marginalized communities in contributing to the global dialogue on the crisis of global warming. The politicization of global warming debates seems to almost exclusively shut out the voices of activists, indigenous communities, and faith leaders from the debates on what to do about global warming and the environment, or on the legitimacy of the debate itself. In either case, the voiceless have much to tell us about the care and nurture of the planet, and what it means to live in harmony with the earth and with each other.

Native American communities, and indigenous cultures around the world, have found creative ways to live in harmony with the planet, and have delved into the mysteries of sustainability and flourishing in all dimensions of human life.

They remind us that the ecological crisis is real and poses a challenge to what it means for the church to remain faithful to the call of God in Jesus Christ today. The situation is bleak, as the following data reveal:

1. More than a billion people (three times the population of the entire European Union) live in absolute poverty, living on less than a dollar a day.
2. About 2 billion people do not have access to drinking water.
3. 100 million people (equivalent to the combined population of France, Spain, and Belgium) are homeless.
4. 800 million people live in a state of famine.
5. 150 million children, up to the age of five, suffer from malnutrition.
6. Every year 14 million children die before they are five days old.[18]

These stark conditions cannot be divorced from the condition of the environment. I think Latin American theologian Leonardo Boff is correct:

> Human beings increasingly discover themselves as part of nature, a member of the community of life. The relation between a human being and nature cannot be a relation of dominion; rather, it must be a relation of co-living in an alliance of fraternity, respect and dialogue. Human beings require nature to provide for their needs, and at the same time, nature, which has been marked by human cultures, needs human beings so that it can be preserved, maintained, and able to recover its equilibrium. All beings in nature are subjects with rights, because in their own way, they are carriers of information and of subjectivity. On this ground, everything that exists and lives deserves to exist and live.[19]

The biblical affirmation that the "earth is the Lord's and the fullness thereof" is a clarion call for people of faith to heed the call for justice in the care of the planet and its resources. The fate of human beings is uniquely tied to the fate of the planet. The Bible is explicit in the ways in which God's redemptive love and concern for humanity are intricately related to the existential conditions on the planet as well.

The tragic costs of the industrial age, matched with the intensification of globalization as an economic and political reality that privileges profit and wealth over against human flourishing and respect for God's creation, invite a radical call for prophetic hope and discipleship to Jesus Christ in our time. The effects of "greenhouse" gases and the rise of pollu-

18. Boff, *Global Civilization*, 48.
19. Boff, *Global Civilization*, 58.

tion that depletes the earth's natural resources — problems facing God's creation — present a moment of prophetic and spiritual discernment as to the call of the church and all believers for our time. On almost every continent in the world, the ravages of injustice — poverty; HIV/AIDS; health-related epidemics, from malaria to diphtheria — are almost always connected to the lack of sustainable and renewable resources related to both the conditions and the ownership of land.

Rethinking the doctrine of creation and the shared distinction between humans and the environment is a necessary point of departure in connecting the quest for justice and human dignity with the healing of the land (constructive approaches to the environmental crisis). Psalm 24's declaration that "the earth is the Lord's and the fullness thereof" echoes the biblical affirmation that God is sovereign and holds dominion over all living things and the created world. God is creator and sustainer over all life and reality. God is the self-perpetuating, self-created, all-wise, eternal God who creates as a consequence of God's love, power, justice, and wisdom. God is God of all life and reality — all lands, social and political systems, peoples, cultures, the waters and fruits of the earth. The classical doctrine of creation says that the God who reveals God's self in Jesus Christ is Lord of all creation, including social and political systems and global capitalistic systems (i.e., multinational corporations, and organizations such as the International Monetary Fund, the World Bank, and the United Nations). Capitalism, which has indeed fueled untold wealth for Western nations, as an economic system, has contributed to the massive depletion of the earth's resources, rugged individualism, and an unmitigated culture of materialism and consumption, of which many Christians (especially in the Western world) have been held captive. The church, and hearing the Spirit of God in our time, does not occur in isolation but takes place in a hostile world of materialism and greed where human desire (what we think we want and need) is now manufactured by the incessant engines of sophisticated marketing strategies and technologies of desire.

The sovereignty and reign of God are not limited to the particular ecclesial traditions of the church; God is the God of all creation, which means the call of the gospel is to serve as a gift to all creation, to serve as a clarion call for God's call of restoration, healing, transformation, and wholeness in the world. All around the world, Christians are realizing that care and concern for the planet are directly tied to the quest for justice and human dignity in the world, especially concerning the poor concentrated in the global South. Much of the theological justification for distinguishing the fate of the planet and the human condition, which allows for a view that says since we live in a fallen world, God is only concerned about the souls of human beings (less about the body and the material world in which humans exist), emerges out of a colonial, imperial theology that is still reflected in many of our churches, ecumenical bodies, and faith communions. The colonial or imperial theologies, emerging out of the eighteenth and nineteenth centuries, retreated dramatically away from the idea that God's redemption speaks to both the body and the soul — spiritual and material realities.

Desmond Tutu said it best in speaking about the early colonial presence in South Africa. He said when the European explorers came to the shores, they (the Africans) had the land and the Europeans had the Bible. So, he said, "they prayed, and when they opened their eyes, the Europeans had the land and they had the Bible." The antiapartheid struggle in South Africa was as much about the quest for human dignity and justice as it was about returning the land to its rightful place in God's economy — where all of God's people are free to flourish spiritually, materially, socially, and politically.

Because the poor need adequate food and clean water, the ways in which Christians, particularly Baptists, think about ecological issues must be grounded in the persistent quest for justice, which includes not only fair and equitable distribution of the earth's resources but also access to modern medicine, shelter, education, and a world free of violence and domination. In Zimbabwe; Chiapas, Mexico; Kenya; and the United States, there is an emerging awareness that the environmental crisis is the key issue of faith communities around the world — not simply because as creator, God is concerned about the environment, but because in God's call to redeem and save humanity (calling the world back to God's self), God is also issuing the call to heal the land as well. Hearing the Spirit in our time means hearing the call for justice and its deeply rooted connection with the environment. In particular, Wangari Muta Maathai's movement in Kenya is but one example of the kinds of creative witnesses that are occurring in our time.

Wangari Muta Maathai was born in Nyeri, Kenya, in 1940. The first woman in East and Central Africa to earn a doctorate, Wangari Maathai obtained a degree in biological sciences from Mount St. Scholastica College in Atchison, Kansas (1964). She subsequently earned a master of science degree from the University of Pittsburgh (1966). She pursued doctoral studies in Germany and at the University of Nairobi, obtaining a Ph.D. (1971) from the latter, where she also taught veterinary anatomy. She became chair of the Department of Veterinary Anatomy and an associate professor in 1976 and 1977, respectively. In both cases, she was the first woman to attain those positions in the region. Wangari Maathai was active in the National Council of Women of Kenya in 1976-87, and was its chairman in 1981-87. While serving in that body she introduced the idea of planting trees with the people in 1976 and continued to develop it into a broad-based, grassroots organization whose main focus is the planting of trees with women's groups in order to conserve the environment and improve their quality of life. Through the Green Belt Movement she has assisted women in planting more than 20 million trees on their farms and on school and church compounds.[20]

Michael Welker argues that the proper point of departure for a biblical theological approach to the doctrine of creation begins with a rereading of Genesis 1 and 2. One must start by challenging the presuppositions guiding the alternatives of "*creatio ex nihilo* and creation out of chaos."[21] Welker questions the notion of "determinacy," by which creation must emerge as a change of form of some preexisting reality, vis-à-vis a process of creating out of chaos, or the act of creating with no preexisting structure or reality. Welker also takes up another dimension of the creation debate that considers the binary opposites of "creation at the beginning *(primordialis)* and '*creatio continua.*'"[22] He observes that "the concept of creation that underlies these alternatives connects images of production and of the exercise of power."[23] The classical doctrine of creation has promoted a conception of divine power on which creation is totally dependent. This sort of approach to the doctrine of creation was captured in James Weldon Johnson's *God's Trombones,* in the African American preaching tradition:

> And God stepped out on space,
> And he looked around and said:
> I'm lonely —
> I'll make me a world.
> And far as the eye of God could see
> Darkness covered everything,

20. http://nobelprize.org/nobel_prizes/peace/laureates/2004/maathai-bio.html.
21. Michael Welker, *Creation and Reality* (Minneapolis: Fortress, 1999), 7.
22. Welker, *Creation and Reality,* 7.
23. Welker, *Creation and Reality,* 8.

Blacker than a hundred midnights
Down in a cypress swamp.

Then God smiled,
And the light broke,
And the darkness rolled up on one side,
And the light stood shining on the other,
And God said: That's good![24]

This approach is echoed by Karl Barth, who holds in tension the delicate dance between creation as a process of God's divine power and the notion of creation's dependence on God for its very being. Welker's key argument in terms of his rereading of Genesis 1 and 2 emphasizes the ways in which God is responding and reacting to that which is already in existence. He writes, "The texts are full of instances that emphasize and develop God's reactive experiencing and acting as God reacts to the presence of what is created. The texts describe in a differentiated way God's intervening in what is already created, intervening for the purpose of further specification."[25]

God's "evaluative perception" leads God to intervene and reconstitute creation in a way that God has seen fit for it to be. God's naming of creation indicates God's desire for clarity, specificity, and meaning of the created order. "And God saw that what had been created was good" (Gen. 1:4a, 10b). The creation account explicitly reserves for the human being — not yet differentiated into man and woman — the naming of "all cattle, the birds of heaven and all animals of the field" (Gen. 2:19-20). The creation account explicitly emphasizes the validity of this fundamental, culture-creating human activity. "And as the human being named each being, so was it to be called" (Gen. 2:19b).[26] At the core of Welker's assertions is the idea that God not only creates and acts in relation to the created order, but God also reacts and responds to what God has laid God's hands upon. Within the nature of creation itself is a process by which human beings are participants in the ongoing process of creation.[27]

The Bible attests to the reality that God's being is "in the heavens" —

24. *The Heath Anthology of American Literature,* vol. 2, 2nd ed. (Lexington, Mass.: Heath, 1994), 1053-55.
25. Welker, *Creation and Reality,* 9.
26. Welker, *Creation and Reality,* 10.
27. Welker, *Creation and Reality,* 10.

above and over against, superior, and in dramatic contrast to human creation. It makes clear that God is not human and the affairs within the life of God are beyond the scope of human capacities. "The talk of God's being in the heavens is to emphasize and inculcate that God and God's action toward the world are not at our disposal and cannot be manipulated."[28] The notion of the "earth" or earthly creation has been viewed as the *oikos* of God, or that space upon which God dwells, yet human beings are invited to serve as stewards over. The *oikos* is related to concepts such as *domus* and polis, which are related systems of understanding the ways in which creation has been ordered. Claus Westermann observed:

> If we look at this story not as enlightened modern men and women who know better about everything, but rather with a readiness to listen, then we will hear something in it that would do our world good to hear. Our mechanized world has little appreciation for animals; we push them to the periphery of our thoughts. But they are creatures, and as such they share in our humanity. We cannot deny them their share without consequence. There is always a point at which animals have a better and sharper alertness than do people. There are moments when it is right and good for people to learn from and heed animals.[29]

To hear God's call for justice and to respond prophetically in our time to the environmental crisis mean challenging those systems and structures (powers and principalities) that stand against the flourishing of human life and God's creation. The recent BP oil spill in the Gulf of Mexico is a small yet compelling dramatization of the problems and challenges globalization poses to the environment. In a postindustrial era, the world is much more interconnected than ever before. Economies and environmental conditions around the world are profoundly fused together by the realities of global commerce, technology, and communications. Because of the economic, political, and social forces of globalization, the church must fight passionately to resist the negative features of globalization and challenge systems of power that marginalize the masses of poor people around the world. Twenty percent of the world's population (primarily in the West) are now using up 80 percent of the world's resources, while 80 per-

28. Welker, *Creation and Reality*, 34.
29. Claus Westermann, *God's Angels Need No Wings*, trans. D. L. Scheidt (Philadelphia: Fortress, 1979), 45. See also Welker's *Creation and Reality*, 49.

cent of the world's population, especially in the global South (Asia, Africa, and Latin America), are consuming less than 20 percent of the world's resources, many living off of less than a dollar a day. It is sad to say that the church (historically and in the present) has often served as handmaiden of the demonic and exploitative forces of capitalism, greed, and the rape of the planet.

Globalization refers to the ever expanding, interconnected decentralization of global economic systems and the massive devastation to the environment caused by the race for rapid economic exchange. These forces invite a prophetic and passionate call for environmental justice in local and global spheres. Carlton Waterhouse makes the compelling observation that

> Globalization produces a variety of effects — some desirable, many not. The undesirable effects, what I call collateral damage accompanying globalization, include economic displacement, ecological destruction, and political estrangement. Economic displacement means that workers no longer have employment opportunities rooted in the life of their local communities. The growth and "development" associated with globalization are often based on the destruction of ecosystems and habitats. Furthermore, development and growth almost always mean the expansion of consumer culture and the proportionate increase in pollution and pollution sources. Politically, globalization means the increased influence of economic entities such as large corporations on local politicians as these entities expand their power and influence into additional markets.[30]

Some practical strategies that people of faith might consider in the quest to live faithfully and passionately to "heal the land," for the "earth is the Lord's and the fullness thereof, and all who dwell therein," might be the following:

1. Act locally and think globally! Support community farming.
2. Be responsible consumers with an awareness of the inequities and disparities in the world.
3. Speak prophetically and courageously for environmental justice in

---

30. Carlton Waterhouse, "Engaging Environmental Justice," in *Justice in a Global Economy: Strategies for Home, Community, and World* (Louisville: Westminster John Knox, 2006), 78.

local communities and in terms of international politics (such as the Kyoto treaty and policies that will help resist global warming).

4. Promote solidarity among Christians and cultures across the planet, when the call to Christ and the communion of faith trump national allegiances; tribes; and race, gender, and cultural specificity.

5. Reform global economic and environmental policies. For instance, groups like the Jubilee movement and the Oxfam "Make Trade Fair" program are working for more just policies and institutions.

6. Challenge our own assumptions about what it means to be "Christian"; go beyond those perspectives that simply maintain the status quo and current inequities. There must be a growing recognition that the affluent and Christians in the wealthiest nations have a stake in the struggle for justice in terms of social, political, and economic transformation.

Prophetic Rage and the New Struggle for Freedom

The ecological crisis and the question of sustainability cannot be divorced from the larger problem of poverty. The people and the land are interconnected and bound together. The prophetic task ahead must make connections between the plight of sustaining the land and feeding God's people as well. King recognized that the black experience, in particular, was an entry into the larger, systemic, forces threatening human existence as a whole. King understood this when he turned his attention to the issue of poverty in the mid-1960s. From 1967 to 1968, King and his staff members with the Southern Christian Leadership Conference began planning a national Poor People's Campaign where they would call for a "bill of rights" for the poor. This bill of rights would include universal health care, a guaranteed education and housing program, basic access to food and clothing, and most importantly, jobs for all Americans who desire to work. The plan was to lead a massive pilgrimage of poor people to the nation's capital, and essentially "camp out" until action was taken. Part of the plan was to cripple the federal government by holding round-the-clock protests and sit-ins on the two bridges leading into the capital. Even after King's assassination, Ralph Abernathy, Andrew Young, Wyatt Tee Walker, Coretta King, and others attempted to forge ahead, but the plan was a painful disappointment as a national depression set in, and disillusionment and severe rain dampened the effort.

King's observation about the challenge of dealing with the reality of poverty still speaks in resounding ways today. "The curse of poverty has no justification in our age. It is socially as cruel and blind as the practice of cannibalism at the dawn of civilization, when men ate each other because they had not yet learned to take food from the soil or to consume the abundant animal life around them. The time has come for us to civilize ourselves by the total, direct and immediate abolition of poverty."[31]

Now, in a post–civil rights era, there is a critical need to reassess the nature of the civil rights movement, and King's legacy (in general) for our own time. I would like to offer up a few brief areas that may contribute to a constructive and prophetic vision for black flourishing going into the future. If the black freedom struggle (and perhaps the greater struggle for marginalized peoples of various communities) is to move ahead, we must begin to "think globally and act locally." Improvements in technology, global travel, and mass communication now enable people of faith and the broader public to connect with people around the country and globally in real time. This causes us to reimagine our place in the world and our personal and social responsibilities for helping reshape our communities. The people we work with, the institutions and ideas we are a part of, even our communities of faith, are all global and multicultural in makeup. One of the greatest barriers to building a sense of collective consciousness today is the fact that the black community is more diverse than ever before. Like President Obama, who has both white and black parents, grew up in Hawaii and Indonesia, and was raised largely by his white mother and white grandparents, the social and racial identity of black life today is deeply fragmented and fluid. We must embrace a pluralistic, diverse, and global vision of black life that is expansive, and global. For instance, we must begin to see our connection with our African heritage and ancestry as a basis from which to build a common struggle.

The prophetic task before us today must focus on common values and must have a multidimensional focus. Historically, since 1903 when W. E. B. Du Bois published *The Souls of Black Folks*, collective consciousness and black solidarity have increased the black plight. Black leaders were reluctant to openly challenge other black leaders for fear of alienation or being criticized for undermining black progress. Black politics is much more complex nowadays. For instance, the presidency of Obama is a his-

---

31. Martin Luther King Jr., *Where Do We Go from Here: Chaos or Community?* (reprint, Eugene, Ore.: Wipf and Stock, 2002), 193.

torical triumph when we think about the history of slavery, racism, and Jim Crow segregation (where as recently as the mid-1960s blacks were denied the vote in many cities across the South). So, blacks as well as whites have much cause to celebrate in terms of Obama's election and presidency. However, when Obama stood up to take the oath of office to protect and defend the Constitution of the United States from enemies foreign and domestic on January 20, 2009, he became intertwined with the principalities and powers that govern the entrenched political systems in the nation. Whatever prophetic matters were on Barack Obama's mind as he ran for office and served as a community organizer were replaced with the biblical mantle of "king," or the one who governs. As Peter Paris observed, and as is reflected in the Old Testament tradition of the prophets, the king can never be prophet, nor can the prophet be king. So the prophetic role of the church, and Christian believers in general, is to speak truth to power, whether that power comes as a black and brown face, or whether that power comes in white skin. The prophetic task means to continue to work toward establishing God's ways of being in the world.

Also, the prophetic task means thinking and acting with a generational consciousness. Johann Wolfgang von Goethe, the German philosopher and poet, once observed that the "destiny of any nation rests in the hands of its young people." There is an ancient Native American proverb that says, "The land does not belong to us, it is merely borrowed from our children." We must move swiftly, with prophetic urgency, in cultivating leaders for the present and future generations. Currently, there is not only a crisis of leadership in the black community. There is also a crisis of black intellectualism, which in recent years has grossly neglected the task of black leadership. Part of this is accounted for by the class divide in the black community, and part is due to the structural nature of higher education, which still leans toward a Eurocentric, privileged system that favors a ruling-class orientation.

Finally, the black community, and certainly the wider church as well, must confront our own complacency in a culture of consumption and materialism, and the justice issues that create new forms of pseudoslavery. Slavoj Žižek once raised the provocative question, "Why do we continue to want what we do not need, and need what we do not want?" The black community and its leaders must begin to think critically about the ways we participate in our own oppression by participating in a culture of materialism and unending consumption. Likewise, we must challenge the economic disparities that continue to plague poor communities in this country and abroad. This would involve tracing the economic connections linked to mass incarceration, unemployment, housing issues, and public education. We must create connections and relationships with diverse groups (Latinos/Latinas, Asians, whites, etc.) to advance a common beloved community of justice, peace, freedom, and equality for all.

Reclaiming the Prophetic

The tradition of prophetic Christianity still represents one of the most powerful aspects of the Christian narrative. It is the element of Christianity that demands constant renewal and reform, that refuses to rest with doctrines and creeds alone, but calls for immediate and unrequited justice, love, peace, healing, and reconciliation in God's creation. Jean-Jacques Rousseau, the Franco-Swiss philosopher of the Enlightenment, said that "human beings are born free, but everywhere they find themselves in shackles." It has been true historically, and is God's will, that human beings live free — as self-determined autonomous agents of their own existence, relating to God not as slaves but as agents of love, peace, truth, and justice in God's creation. Freedom is rooted in God and is a birthright from God. However, there is also the human, worldly propensity to enslave, dominate, control, and exploit. The task of civil society, even organizing social, political, and economic institutions, is to reflect and approximate the kind of freedom that God desires in human creation.

Today, even with all our economic, political, and perhaps even religious prosperity, we still seem to be enslaved to a multitude of forces. Enslavement takes on many forms. It may be physical, psychological, economic, or spiritual. One of the chief ways in which human beings have been enslaved, historically, has been through the tentacles of political and economic systems, embodied in great empires and nation-states around the world. In many ways, as much as we (you and I) would like to think that we have some measure of freedom, life outcomes are often determined by the historical moments in which we live, our geographic or social location, or simply as a function of our family experiences. Life is often impacted by generational factors that shape the choices we are challenged to navigate on a daily basis. Why do we live in an age where education is no guarantee of economic prosperity and stability; where doing good may leave us destitute; where wrong seems to be right, and up seems to be down; where schoolteachers can't find decent wages, and Wall Street fat cats have money to blow? Why is a child growing up in Southside Chicago, the Bronx, Watts, Soweto, Nairobi, and Somalia ten times more likely to live in poverty or die of gun violence than the kid growing up in the Hamptons, Martha's Vineyard, Buckhead, or Brentwood?

The challenges we face are not simply political or economic; they are also psychological and spiritual. Cornel West makes the stirring observation that "the notion that black people are human beings is a relatively new discovery in the modern West."[32] For the better part of Western history, and perhaps up until the revolutionary spirit of the 1960s and early 1970s, it was normative to think that black people and people of color around the world were physically, socially, morally, and intellectually inferior to Europeans. Eurocentrism, a perspective that situates the Western world as the center of God's creation, continued to inform destructive systems of colonialism, slavery, apartheid, Nazism, and fascism around the world. And although many of the structures undergirding these systems were dismantled by the fervent, passionate, and courageous cries of freedom fighters around the world, the messages and themes of these systems live on.

These systems live on in the privileging of European culture, its values, art, music, literature, thought, and ways of being as normative for all other cultures on the globe. They live on in the subliminal messages of white supremacy included within the theologies, ideologies, and philosophies popularized in mainstream culture. They live on in unjust economic systems and political institutions such as the International Monetary Fund, the World Bank, the Federal Reserve, and the larger banking institutions in the United States and Europe, where over 90 percent of the world's wealth rests within the hands of a group small enough to fit into a lecture hall. And yet, with and through the power of God operating in the human heart, human beings (as Reinhold Niebuhr reminded us) have the capacity to transcend their immediate social, political, economic, or even religious circumstances. Although we have the ability to sink down to the depths of hell, we also have the ability to transcend and reach up to the heavenly angelic heights. After all, we are made but "a little lower than the angels," as the Eighth Psalm says.

The release of this tension may very well rest with how we understand the relationship between God (the activity and the life of God) and Caesar. In a casual manner, Jesus was asked whether it was right or lawful to give taxes to "Caesar." He asked to see a coin, and the coin he was shown

32. *The Cornel West Reader* (New York: Basic Civitas Books, 1999), 70.

had, on one side, an image of the head of the reigning emperor, Tiberius Caesar. Images of emperors regularly appeared on the currencies of the empire. As we know, there is no state without a national currency. The food and blood of empire is money. Empire needs it to live, to breathe, to gain strength. Through the process of taxation, it also serves as a show of allegiance and faithfulness to the imperial cause. In short, Caesar's coin is a symbol of empire and the ways in which imperialism serves as a stabilizing narrative for what it means to be human.

So, when Jesus was presented with this piercing question, he was being asked, in effect, who should have our ultimate allegiance, as people of faith on the quest for truth, and how do we resist the lure and clutches of imperial bondage, which forms of currency and exchange represent? The Roman Empire promulgated a sort of "Roman imperial theology" based on violence, power, domination, and material prosperity. It was an imperial vision of the world that defined life (and living) as a quest for domination, power, control, violence as a path to peace, or a quest for the *Pax Romana* (peace of Rome). Violence was and continues to be the language of empire. As Crossan points out, the natural sequence of Roman imperial theology was "religion, war, victory, and peace."

It seems that what Jesus was ultimately calling for in this passage was resistance — resistance, perhaps, in three dimensions. The first was economic, political, and social resistance to the multiple forms of domination represented by Caesar's coin. "Render therefore to Caesar the things that are Caesar's, and to God the things that are God's" (Matt. 22:17 NKJV). I don't think Jesus was saying that Christians should not pay taxes or serve as good law-abiding citizens of the nation-state. What he was clearly calling for was an awareness of their ultimate allegiance to God, over all else. Because, ultimately, everything that belongs to Caesar belongs to God, since "the earth is the Lord's and the fullness thereof."

As creator and sustainer of the universe, God is God over all spheres of human life. There are no places and spaces where God is not God. God is intimately related to all aspects of human creation. And although God is not in the world as in substance, because God would be God even if heaven and earth passed away, God's love and justice and truth still call to the world in all ways, bringing it back into relationship with God. It was a compelling declaration that ultimately Caesar (that is, the state or any political or social institution that gains its power by and through the state) must yield to the activity of God in the world. "Render therefore to Caesar the things that are Caesar's, and to God the things that are God's," Jesus says. In these simple words, Jesus is saying that, on the one hand, what belongs to Caesar is Caesar's and must be understood as such. Caesar can be associated with that part of our earthly existence that deals with concrete materiality, capitalism, consumerism, domination, conquest, and violence. These forces are a self-contained reality in and of themselves. On the other hand, the things of Caesar (particularly the state or worldly systems) must not be confused with God. God is separate and distinct from the world. And yet, the world belongs to God, and even Caesar and the things of Caesar are subject to God's power and authority. And if God is a God of love, if God is a God of truth and justice, of peace and compassion, of forgiveness and joy, then the world that God wills for human beings is what Martin Luther King called the "beloved community," Desmond Tutu called "the rainbow people of God," and Maria Asasi-Diaz called the "kinship of God's people."

Therefore, our task is to usher in God's freedom and justice, healing, and love in the world. David Walker, in his 1829 address known as "Walker's Appeal," called on abolitionists and enslaved Africans alike to rise up and claim their freedom as an inherent right from God. Frederick Douglass would echo these calls when he said, "Without struggle there is no progress. Those who profess to favor freedom yet deprecate agitation are like men [and women] who want the harvest without plowing the fields, rain without thunder and lightning, they want the ocean without the aweful roar of its many waters."[33] There can be no progress without struggle, was his refrain.

The call for political and economic resistance was felt in the church's resistance to slavery, Dietrich Bonhoeffer's witness against Nazism in Germany, the struggle against apartheid in South Africa, the civil rights struggle for desegregation and voting rights, and perhaps even today with the fight to abolish the death penalty, for human rights to end poverty, and for sustainability of the planet. It is still our call today — to challenge unjust systems, be they economic, political, or religious. Our call is to proclaim God's freedom and justice in the world, liberation and dignity for the marginalized and downtrodden bodies of the earth.

Perhaps the second form of resistance Jesus was calling for was psychological, a sort of internal resistance to imperialism. What was really at stake in Jesus' response was not simply a political declaration akin to the

33. Frederick Douglass, "West India Emancipation" (speech delivered at Canandaigua, N.Y., August 3, 1857).

American Revolution's call for independence from British tyranny, but also a declaration of identity. One of the most powerful lures of empire is the guarantee of national identity, of grounding one's sense of self in a larger narrative about the world. Caesar's coin, and allegiance to Caesar's coin, was an invitation to identification with Caesar and the "things" of Caesar. Identity and sense of self could be wrapped up and encased within Caesar, the things of Caesar, the things that Caesar's coin could attain — material realities and prosperity, power, domination, worldly pleasure. Caesar's coin had the power to enslave, to kill, to starve, to maim, to build kingdoms and fortresses, to attain and maintain mighty armies.

The counter to giving Caesar what is Caesar's is to give God what belongs to God. For in God is the power to liberate, to redeem social systems and unjust political structures, to fight against tyranny in all its forms. For social, political, and economic systems function out of ideologies, theologies, and philosophies that inform practices and human behavior. Before institutions, even nation-states, are formed, they are born in the hearts and imaginations of human beings, launched deep within the wells of the subconscious, tearing through the walls of human experience and interpretation of those experiences to make sense of life as we know it. One of the most troubling aspects of black life today has to do with the ways in which black identity has become so intertwined with capitalism, consumerism, and whiteness as normative cultural standards of living and being in the world. At the root of the impulse to be consumed in capitalism and consumerism (or the bling-bling culture, the good life) is the threat of nihilism and meaninglessness.

What we are most afraid of is nothingness, the absence of meaning or substance, the abyss of nonbeing. So the story of materialism, capitalism, and consumerism is the sales pitch of meaning — that things translate into meaning. This is to say, if you don't have this or that, then you are nothing or a nobody. By the mid-1960s, during the civil rights movement and black power movement, the rising cry was black consciousness, and more broadly the forging of a collective consciousness. It is sad today to think about how we have lost that deep sense of consciousness to systemic oppression and the ways in which it leads us to participate in our own oppression. What we need today is more than simply a rise of black consciousness; we need a sort of economic, and political, and cultural consciousness to systems of domination — economic, political, social, and religious.

Conclusion

Reclaiming the *prophetic,* as opposed to being seduced by the thirst for profits and wealth, means confronting nihilism with hope and resistance. The greatest problem we have is overcoming the kind of internalized self-hatred and nihilism based on the feeling of powerlessness as a function of racial oppression in our society. So, in effect, we hate our brothers and sisters because deep inside we really hate ourselves. As a culture, we have allowed much of our identity to be intertwined with material prosperity, violence, domination, and conquest (or simply Caesar's coin). These have infiltrated our churches, blinded our children, distorted our imagination, and robbed us of vision and purpose in the world. But internal resistance means claiming our place in God, locating our identity in the life of God; remembering who we are and whose we are; that we are made in the *imago Dei* (image of God), shaped in the *imago Christi* (the image of Christ), and called to live as free, moral, and powerful agents of God's transformation in the world. As Howard Thurman would say, sometimes we must remind ourselves and others that we are somebody; that our value comes not from the car we drive, or the house we live in, or the shoes we wear, or the size of our church, or the scope of our family center, but from God!

Finally, perhaps the most dynamic form of resistance to empire is spiritual resistance. Spiritual resistance, rooted in the life of God, is what permeates, inspires, and sustains all other forms of resistance and overcoming in the world. Teilhard de Chardin said we are not physical beings trying to be spiritual but "spiritual" beings learning what it means to live a material existence in the world. The most piercing dimension of the Gospel passage is when Jesus says, "Give unto God what is God's." That is a very compelling and provocative statement because it begs the question of exactly what belongs to God; what are the things of God; what do we owe God? Some wish to make a sharp distinction between the things of God and the things of "Caesar's coin." But to the ancient minds of the hearers of these words, there was no distinction. There was an embedded connection because of the understanding that God was and is creator and sustainer of the universe. That the earth is the Lord's and the fullness thereof and all who dwell therein. So what God ultimately desires is that we render our all and our everything to God. That whatever is in the world and of the world should be subject to the will and way of God.

Ultimately, the prophetic call for global justice means placing human life and the earth as the end of any economic system. It means celebrating the flourishing of all creation as the grounds for building and forging a new global economy, one free of exploitation and mass poverty, that does not destabilize the lives of all but ensures stability, growth, equality, and freedom for all.

There is a wonderful hymn of the black religious experience that captures this well:

> All to Jesus I surrender;
> all to him I freely give;
> I will ever love and trust him,
> in his presence daily live.
>
> All to Jesus I surrender;
> Lord, I give myself to thee;
> fill me with thy love and power;
> let thy blessing fall on me.
>
> *(Refrain)*
> All to Jesus I surrender;
> now I feel the sacred flame.
> O the joy of full salvation!
> Glory, glory, to his name!

CHAPTER FIVE

Dark Waters

Every time I feel the Spirit moving in my heart, I will pray.[1]

From the darkness cometh the light.[2]

Prophetic rage also means offering creative and dynamic resources for confronting empire and nihilism. If social transformation is to occur, whether in the form of cultural change, economic transformation, or spiritual renewal, we must take seriously the beauty and power of black artistic expression, activism, and spirituality as forms of resistance and prophetic imagination. In his *Darkwater: Voices from within the Veil,* W. E. B. Du Bois testifies to the ways in which black people confronted the horrors of slavery and the deep and pervasive meaninglessness of American racism through the genius and ingenuity of black cultural expression.[3] In *The Souls of Black Folks,* Du Bois reminds us that black people fought off the demons of meaninglessness and despair by digging deep within the well-

---

1. "Every Time I Feel the Spirit," Negro spiritual.
2. Lucy A. Delaney, "From the Darkness Cometh the Light or Struggles for Freedom," in *Six Women's Slave Narratives,* gen. ed. Henry Louis Gates (New York: Oxford University Press, 1988). The piece was originally published by the publishing house of J. T. Smith (St. Louis).
3. W. E. B. Du Bois, *Darkwater: Voices from within the Veil,* introduction by Manning Marable (Mineola, N.Y.: Dover Publications, 1999; original New York: Harcourt, Brace and Co., 1920).

spring of hope and love that emerged from unimaginable suffering and grief. Du Bois proclaimed that mining the inner world of "work and wealth," of "beauty and death" from the perspective of black folk, may very well pave the way for overcoming the threat of nihilism embedded in a culture of imperialism and consumerism today. For instance, through the spirituals, black folks called on the God who could make a way out of no way, the God that guided them through deep rivers and on into campground. As in "Deep River," which declared in a slow, melodious rhythm:

> Deep river, my home is over Jordan,
> Deep river, Lord, I want to cross over into campground,
> Lord, I want to cross over into campground,
> Lord, I want to cross over into campground,
> Oh chillun, oh, don't you want to go, — to that gospel feast,
> That promised land, that land, where all is peace?[4]

The spirituals, birthed from the visceral and gut-wrenching anguish of human suffering, not only provided a means of coded communication among slaves beyond the watchful ear of their masters, they also provided a soul language, a prophetic language of dissonance and subversiveness. They created a space for self-expression and agency that allowed the enslaved to cry out in the face of injustice, pain, and powerlessness. They were otherwise silenced by the stinging whip of oppression, but the spirituals gave voice to their pain and became the liberating force that broke the chains of enslavement, disarming the powers and principalities of imperialism and domination.

The power and creativity needed to resist the seductive problems of modernity's preoccupation with categories and distinctions were further thickened during the Harlem Renaissance, when figures like Langston Hughes began to claim a new sense of black personhood and cultural awareness. Poems like "The Negro Speaks of Rivers" demonstrated the eloquent beauty and strength of looking back to move forward. They showed that in order to fight nihilism and empire, one must draw on a heritage of overcoming, of resisting, of fighting, of praying, of hoping, of enduring. Langston Hughes wrote:

4. "Deep River," arranged by J. Rosamond Johnson to Booker T. Washington, in James Weldon Johnson, *The Book of American Negro Spirituals* (New York: Viking Press, 1925).

I've known rivers as ancient as the world and older than the flow of
human blood in human veins.
My soul has grown deep like the rivers.[5]

By drawing on what Howard Thurman refers to as "head and heart,"
black peoples throughout the African diaspora were able to find resources
for hope, endurance, and resistance amid a world of terror and death. As in
the context of slavery, the Harlem Renaissance, and Jim Crow segregation,
nihilism seeps into the subconscious self to destroy a sense of purpose and
meaning. It attacks future hopes and possibilities through a denial of existence, through the negation of life. History and heritage, and the ways in
which God reveals God's self through the crucible of human experience,
become a source of hope and resistance for confronting present challenges
as well.

Spirituals such as "Steal Away to Jesus" offered a compelling look at
the brutality of slavery and remained a constant source of renewal and sustenance in confronting the violence of empire and racial oppression in
America.

Steal away, steal away,
Steal away, to Jesus.
Steal away, steal away home,
I ain't got long to stay here.[6]

Following a similar theme of liberation and justice, "Go Down, Moses" speaks to the deep yearning of the enslaved to be free, to resist with
prophetic rage and faithful determination under the weight of empire:

Go down, Moses
'Way down in Egypt land,
Tell ole Pharaoh,
Let my people go.[7]

Other spirituals, like "Git On Board, Little Chillen," "Gwinter Sing
All Along De Way," "Who'll Be a Witness for My Lord?" "Where Shall I Be
When De Firs' Trumpet Soun?" and "Peter, Go Ring Dem Bells," all reflect

5. Langston Hughes, "The Negro Speaks of Rivers" (1921).
6. "Steal Away to Jesus," Negro spiritual.
7. "Go Down, Moses," Negro spiritual.

the fact that resistance to empire requires more than mere language. It means calling forth all aspects of the self — mind, body, and spirit — to engage those invisible and persistent powers of violence and dehumanization.

One would search in vain to find a distinctive character to "African American Christianity." In fact, what African American Christianity involves is a complex social, historical, religious, and cultural body of experiences that directly corresponds to African enslavement and the enduring quest for freedom and human dignity.

By pointing out some key features of slave religion and the emergence of the black church before and after Reconstruction, perhaps we can gain a stronger grasp of African American Christianity and the ways it contributes to broader readings of the Christian narrative. Albert J. Raboteau, Sterling Stuckey, Andrew Billingsley, and Lerone Bennett, in addition to sociologists like Du Bois, E. Franklin Frazier, and Melville J. Herskovits, have contributed greatly to the formation and development of the African and African American religious experience.

Raboteau's most definitive book on the subject is *Slave Religion: The "Invisible Institution" in the Antebellum South*.[8] In it Raboteau treats the two primary dimensions of slave religion by examining African diaspora, animism and African deities, and the emergence of Christianity as a merging of Western Judeo-Christianity and African traditional religions and culture in slave life.

According to Raboteau, the tragedy of over ten million Africans taken from their homeland to work as slaves in mines, plantations, and households in the New World is unparalleled in human history. In this event, political, cultural, economic, and family systems were disrupted and fractured. "Tribal and linguistic groups were broken up, either on the coasts of Africa or in the slave pens across the Atlantic" (4). Raboteau argues that in the New World, it was essential to eradicate all vestiges of African culture because it held the power to unify, mobilize, and cause resistance among the enslaved. However, "African beliefs and customs persisted and were transmitted by slaves to their descendents. Shaped and modified by a new environment, elements of African folklore, music, language, and religion were transplanted in the New World by the African diaspora" (4). By the African

8. Albert J. Raboteau, *Slave Religion: The "Invisible Institution" in the Antebellum South* (Oxford: Oxford University Press, 1978). Page references to this work have been placed in the text.

diaspora, Raboteau means the dramatic dispersion of African presence and culture essentially from the fifteenth century onward.

The one major link connecting African past to American present, for Raboteau, was religion. Particularly in the Americas, African religions (though merging into a hybrid form of Christianity) were not merely surviving Africanisms (or cultural aspects of African traditional religions), but continued to "develop as living traditions putting down new roots in new soil, bearing new fruit as unique hybrids of American origin" (4).

The Wolof, Serer, Mandinke, Bambara, Fulani, and Hausa (a tribal group influenced by Islam) were among the chief tribal groups whose members became slaves in the Americas. As Raboteau points out, some of the first white European contacts with Africans were with "black Moors"; these occurred as early as the 1440s with Portuguese traders. Many Africans believed in a "High God, or Supreme Creator of the world and everything in it" (8). The High God was often associated with the sky, and similar to Western forms of Deism, was depicted as a God aloof and somewhat detached from the ordinary life of human beings. On the other hand, the "lesser gods" and "ancestor spirits" were directly engaged with the everyday affairs of human beings; they received the most attention. The High God was viewed as parent or overseer of the lesser gods. With a high regard for natural forces, many of the "lesser gods" were associated with aspects of the natural order — like the Ibo supreme god Chukwu (Chi-Uku, Great Spirit) or what the Yoruba called *orisha*. The work and activity of the spirits and spirit world were at the center of these ancient African religious traditions. For good or bad, the realm of the spirit was integral to human life at every level, "environmental, individual, social, national, and cosmic" (11).

Raboteau points out several key characteristics of these West African traditional religions (which seem to relate uniquely well to the Christian experience that would be encountered later on during enslavement): "Belief in a transcendent, benevolent God, creator and ultimate source of providence; belief in a number of immanent gods, to whom people must sacrifice in order to make life propitious; belief in the power of spirits animating things in nature to affect the welfare of people; belief in priests and others who were expert in practical knowledge of the gods and spirits; belief in spirit possession, in which gods, through their devotees, spoke to men [human beings]" (11).

As Raboteau rightly acknowledges, all West African societies did not exhibit these characteristics. However, there is a sense in which these features firmly reflect the overwhelming majority of West African traditional religions. Here's the key point Raboteau wishes to make: "the religious background of the slaves was a complex system of belief, and in the life of an African community there was a close relationship between the natural and the supernatural, the secular and the sacred" (15).

When Africans encountered Christianity in America, they saw it through the lens of their African experiences. The extent to which Africans held on to their African cultural and religious heritage was debated heavily among Melville Herskovits and E. Franklin Frazier, both sociologists in the early twentieth century. Herskovits argued that Africans did retain many aspects of their African roots even through the deculturation of slave life. On the other hand, Frazier declared that enslavement led to a total negation of African roots in the United States, although he acknowledged that there were surviving Africanisms in the Caribbean and Latin America (52).

Raboteau, by and large, rejects Frazier's claims by suggesting that Africans did incorporate their African religious roots into new Christian practices that later became normative in the development of the black church. He offers examples and maintains that African American practices of baptism by immersion and spirit possession were consistent with traditional West African religious practices.

Conversion to Christianity was considered one of the primary justifications for slavery since the beginning of the Atlantic slave trade. Through catechesis and general instruction, slaves were indoctrinated into the faith. At the beginning, baptism was viewed as a threat to colonists on the view that baptized slaves would be entitled to equal citizenship and membership in the Christian fellowship. However, later on (as early as 1713), baptism was viewed as nonthreatening as long as it did not interfere with the planter's right to maintain the institution of slavery. Because many planters wanted at least one day off from feeding and clothing their slaves, they established "one day a week" for slaves to plant their own food and work on clothing, which was usually Sunday. It also became a day of visitations, worship, dancing, and communal activities. "Between 1790 and 1820, black Episcopalians, Methodists, Baptists, and Presbyterians founded churches and struggled with church leaders to exercise varying degrees of independence from white control."[9]

Out of these activities, the black preacher emerged as a primary

9. Albert J. Raboteau, *Canaan Land: A Religious History of African Americans* (Oxford: Oxford University Press, 2001), 23.

character in the theater of the black church. On the other hand, a more subversive and covert dimension of slave religion also emerged as slaves would meet secretly to experience a more authentic, transparent religious experience (singing, praying, testifying) and to strategize about prospects for freedom and modes of survival. The Great Awakenings, beginning in 1740, had a tremendous impact on both whites and blacks. Both groups were lifted to new levels of religious fervor.[10] For blacks, the "invisible institution" was the folk religion of the slave community, consisting of a creative fusion of their African cultural roots, Western Christianity, and the quest for survival and freedom. The Great Awakenings spawned a new, more passionate religious energy, leading to increased membership of whites and blacks in the same congregations for a while. Many congregations, such as First Baptist Church of Richmond and Bethel Methodist Church in Philadelphia, were mixed bodies (of both black and white).

The growing number of blacks in congregations during and after the Great Awakenings led to an increased awareness of different expectations and needs in church life. It became difficult for white preachers to adapt their messages to both audiences, and with the increasing biblical literacy of blacks, the inevitability of separation arose. As Henry Mitchell observes, in *Black Church Beginnings: The Long-Hidden Realities of the First Years,* the "refusal of whites to share organizational power or control with African Americans, whether slave or free," remained one of the most persistent problems that led to the racial separation of churches in America.[11] The first independent African American church met in Prince George County, Virginia, in 1756. Later established as the Bluestone Church in Lunenburg County, Virginia, the church carried out its ministry for years under the leadership of white preachers named Philip Mulkey and William Murphey. They later scattered because of the pressures of slave life due to sales. Bluestone later became the First Colored Church of Petersburg, established in 1774. Silver Bluff Church of Aiken, South Carolina, is often cast as the "first" formally established independent black congregation.

Perhaps the most notable earliest established congregation came from the withdrawal of African members from St. George's Methodist Episcopal Church, followers of Richard Allen and Absalom Jones, to establish the Bethel AME Church in Philadelphia, in 1787. The trend started by

10. Raboteau, *Canaan Land,* 128.

11. Henry Mitchell, *Black Church Beginnings: The Long-Hidden Realities of the First Years* (Grand Rapids: Eerdmans, 2004), 54.

Jones and Allen continued throughout the eighteenth century, and through the nineteenth as well.

Countee Cullen's "Heritage" reflects this sentiment:

What is Africa to me:
Copper sun or scarlet sea,
Jungle star or jungle track,
Strong bronzed men, or regal black
Women from whose loins I sprang
When the birds of Eden sang?
One three centuries removed
From the scenes his fathers loved,
Spicy grove, cinnamon tree,
What is Africa to me?[12]

Countee Cullen's poem, born of the creative dissonance of the Harlem Renaissance and the courageous spirit of black people during this era to claim their full humanity, speaks to a need to make sense of the black experience in light of the larger colonizing systems at work in black life. Black theology today is in a state of peril largely because it lacks a clear understanding of its relevance in the postcolonial context. Although some thinkers have attempted to deal with the critical social and political questions confronting the black church and its followers, one fails to find an adequate perspective that speaks to the condition of hopelessness and despair faced by many blacks today. Roberts, in his *Afrocentric Christianity,* suggests an Afrocentric perspective as an approach for Christian ministry. I wish to further argue that it is not merely a perspective for ministry, but also a theological perspective by which to interpret the activity of God in the context of suffering blacks.

Two dynamic scholars, Cheikh Anta Diop and Molefi Kete Asante, have essentially changed the way we think of Africa, its place in the human experience, and the cultural identity of people of African descent throughout the world. We will examine their arguments in an effort to seriously consider the idea of Afrocentrism as a theological perspective. Though the contexts of Diop and Asante are quite different, they share an overarching passion to place Africa back in its rightful place in the human family as embodying a rich and noble heritage intellectually and culturally. Diop

12. Countee Cullen, "Heritage," in *My Soul's High Song: The Collected Writings of Countee Cullen* (New York: Anchor Books, 1991), 52-55.

confronts this task by means of archaeological, anthropological, and scientific tools to affirm that Africa is the "cradle of humanity" — an understanding that is interlocked with the developments of Egypto-Nubian civilizations of the ancient world. Diop provides the historical and intellectual foundation necessary to produce what Asante has coined "Afrocentrism." While Asante draws heavily on the works of Diop, he goes further by naming the significance of cultural identity for liberation and progress, particularly within the African American context. Asante highlights language and how we use it as one of the primary methods of attaining an Afrocentric perspective, and in so doing move toward true freedom.

African theologies have much to teach us about overcoming the problem of nihilism and systems of empire. In fact, the rise of Western imperialism emerges in the late fifteenth century through the ravishing of black bodies and black lands with Western expansionism presumably for "God and gold." The transatlantic slave trade has had devastating and long-lasting impacts throughout the world with the African diaspora and throughout the continent of Africa as well. The Berlin Conference (1884-85) was established at the request of Otto von Bismarck to resolve disputes over the control of Africa's resources. Leaders from countries such as Germany, Great Britain, France, the Netherlands, Portugal, Russia, Spain, Sweden-Norway, and Turkey lobbied and negotiated for how the African continent would be colonized.

Emmanuel Martey has offered perhaps the most definitive study of African religious and theological views, with a unifying synthesis of the multiple traditions, cultures, languages, and nations. In *African Theology: Inculturation and Liberation,* he says:

> The African search for authentic and prophetic theology has at once been a rejection of the dominant Western theological paradigms and an acceptance of African realities and worldview in theological hermeneutics. Consequently in Black Africa, African theology and South African Black theology have come to represent two different schools of theological hermeneutics. They are therefore not synonymous. Expressed respectively in terms of "inculturation" (or "Africanization" or "indigenization") and "liberation," there has thus been a tension or polarity between these two theological traditions since the early 1970s.[13]

13. Emmanuel Martey, *African Theology: Inculturation and Liberation* (Maryknoll, N.Y.: Orbis, 1993), xi.

Major works such as Gwinyai Muzorewa's *Origins and Development of African Theology,* Josiah Young's *Black and African Theologies: Siblings or Distant Cousins?,* Bonganjola Goba's *Agenda for Black Theology: Hermeneutics for Social Change,* and Dwight Hopkins's *Black Theology USA and South Africa: Politics, Culture, and Liberation* have all helped to establish clear distinctions and commonalities between the experiences and struggles of Africans and Africans in America.[14]

In *Afrocentric Christianity,* Roberts argues that Afrocentrism, as a philosophical outlook, provides a means for interpreting, challenging, and overcoming the lingering legacy of colonizing and imperialistic forms of theology. It does so precisely because it offers a prophetic critique among dissonant voices within the broader context of the African and African American religious tradition, of colonialism, empire, and racialized oppression in particular.

Unlike classical perspectives on the interaction of Christianity and empire (see Kwok Pui-lan's *Empire and the Christian Tradition*), Afrocentrism creates the space for inclusion of a multitude of radical voices that have influenced Christian understandings of faith and resistance in modern times. Afrocentrism has also articulated the ways in which communities of resistance, or marginalized bodies, have banded together to struggle against systemic and structural forms of domination in America and throughout the African diaspora. I draw on the notion of Afrocentrism to offer a critique of systems of patriarchy and sexism, particularly as it relates to the marginality of women and LGBTQ persons throughout the African diaspora. Understanding the forces at work in the African diaspora as it relates to issues of both patriarchy and sexism, as well as the history of struggle and resistance to slavery, helps inform the ways in which prophetic rage offers a compelling response to the imperialism and nihilism of Western culture.

Confronting Nihilism with Art

My chief argument here is that Afrocentrism is not just for black people. Because it involves an essential episode in the great melodrama of struggle, resistance, and hope in the human experience, it becomes a resource in claiming new forms of resistance for marginalized bodies around the

14. Martey, *African Theology,* 3.

world. Specifically, the sort of prophetic rage exhibited in the militant voices of figures like Marcus Garvey, Malcolm X, Stokely Carmichael (Kwame Ture), leaders within the Black Panther party, amazing literary artists of the Harlem Renaissance, and the Negritude movement of Paris in the early twentieth century, all bear witness to "hope-in-praxis" and the manner in which prophetic rage (or righteous indignation and struggle) provides the impetus to push back the demons of meaninglessness embedded in postmodern culture. Afrocentrism, as a philosophical perspective and outlook, offers a prophetic critique of the hegemonic forces at work in the Western philosophical tradition that has been and continues to be preoccupied with categories, binaries, distinctions, and descriptions. Afrocentrism suggests that the African experience emphasizes connectivity, relationality, community, where thought and action are inseparable. "Hope" becomes inextricably linked to action, resistance, struggle, and protest. There is no hope apart from prophetic action. There is no hope separate and distinct from the will to fight.

Afrocentrism is an intellectual and cultural movement, led chiefly by Molefi Asante. Asante is a forerunner of postcolonial discourse, linked to British and Caribbean anticolonial figures such as Édouard Glissant, Aimé Césaire, Stuart Hall, and others. The American-born Asante is a former Baptist minister and scholar who became discontented with the ways in which the black church has become co-opted by the forces of empire and colonizing ideas that privilege Western culture and its philosophical tradition over against traditions and cultures of Africa, Asia, and Latin America.

Invoking the experiences and perspectives of men like W. E. B. Du Bois, Marcus Garvey, Malcolm X, and others, Asante has provided a new and intriguing paradigm by which to understand black cultural identity and self-understanding. The strengths and weaknesses of Asante's and Diop's proposals will be examined as well as their continuity and discontinuity in a historical perspective. Are we seeing a new proposal or merely a reformulation of past ideas and thoughts? If new, what is its place in understanding our cultural identity and what impact could it have on problems of self-esteem, a sense of peoplehood, and common destiny experienced by African peoples? By developing a proper understanding of what Asante means by Afrocentrism and Diop's proposal, we might gain a firm insight into these questions and others not presented.

Asante does not ignore the contributions of major African American historical figures that have helped shape the Afrocentric outlook.

Among these are Booker T. Washington, Marcus Garvey, Martin Luther King Jr., Elijah Muhammad, W. E. B. Du Bois, and Malcolm X (who's given the most consideration). Though it is problematic for some of Asante's critics like Delores S. Williams, who points out the inherent sexism within Asante's Afrocentric proposal, Asante credits these men with paving the way for the Afrocentric outlook. Each activist-scholar contributed in some way to its conception. For instance, Booker T. Washington's practical philosophy of economic independence and his emphasis on work and education are key elements to the African cultural project. Washington's mistake, according to Asante, was detaching economic independence from cultural independence. For Asante, the two are indivisible. Without cultural power, economic power is meaningless in Asante's view. Although there were many cultural and intellectual events in the African American experience, we shall examine only the contributions of Malcolm X and the Negritude movement alongside the Harlem Renaissance movement in relation to the Afrocentric perspective as presented by Molefi Kete Asante.

Malcolm X and Black Nationalism

Perhaps no other figure in the history of the African American experience more typifies the meaning of prophetic rage than Malcolm X. Though cast as a militant and radical, Malcolm X was profoundly devout and spiritual. His righteous indignation and outcry against racial injustice on the streets of Harlem and around the world emerged from his deep and fundamental belief that God created each individual with dignity and worth. He refused to accept the presuppositions about the inferiority of black life and white supremacy. He urged blacks to stand up and fight, to claim their inherent rights of citizenship and freedom. He contributed numerous ways to fight for liberation and formulated creative new ideologies that have challenged historical ignorance and political assertions of racial supremacy in America. Whether or not he reached the destination of absolute Afrocentrism is unclear, but Malcolm X did contribute a myriad of ways to resist empire and fight oppression. This element of Asante's construct is significant in that it seems to provide a framework on the nationalistic landscape.

Malcolm X's ideology provides ways to understand the varied class distinctions within the black community and ways of reexamining the practice of Eurocentric thought and behavior. The immense degree of consciousness stimulated through Malcolm X is what is most appealing to Asante's Afrocentric outlook. Both Diop and Asante seem to encourage this collective consciousness of a common historical experience of oppression and also a shared destiny. Diop proposes that this feeling of a shared past will be the glue that holds African peoples together, and by knowing it they have security against the ideological forces of Western imperialism. Asante holds that this shared history is what informs and directs their collective consciousness and leads to productive responses to political and social injustices.

Since Afrocentricity is essentially a philosophical outlook determined by history, there is some discontinuity with Malcolm X's theoretical position. Malcolm X, at his nationalistic height, was a separatist and exclusivist. However, Afrocentrism appreciates and respects other cultures. The Afrocentric idea seems to suggest that one can live alongside a Eurocentric person; however, it is important for the Afrocentric person to be grounded historically and culturally. Malcolm X, especially in his earlier years, saw Eurocentric culture in American society as demonic. Hence, Afro-Americans should separate from that culture to form an independent state. Asante holds that Afrocentrism is a philosophical perspective that can exist within a multicultural setting and still thrive. Nonetheless, the contributions of Malcolm X and the black nationalist movement are indispensable to Asante's intellectual and cultural project.

Negritude Movement

Another key historical movement that has informed the Afrocentric outlook is the Negritude movement — a form of "black consciousness" and feeling of peoplehood with African peoples throughout the world. A term first coined by the Martinician poet and statesman Aimé Césaire in Paris in the 1930s through discussions with fellow students Léopold Sédar Senghor and Léon-Gontran Damas, Negritude represents a historical movement in the African diasporic identity and culture. The meaning and themes found in Negritude are grounded in the thought of people like Martin Delany, William Blyden, and W. E. B. Du Bois. In the French-speaking Caribbean, some politicians early in the twentieth century, like Hégésippe Légitimus, René-Boisneuf, and Gratien Candace, recognized the necessity for blacks to be seen as equals in the global community. This motivation led to exciting conversations among scholars and activists, especially in the Caribbean, about the true meaning of Negritude and its place in the black experience throughout the world.

Historically, Negritude has had two competing interpretations, by the two fellows who coined the term. First, Aimé Césaire has designated the term as seeing the uniqueness and unity of African existence connected historically with contingent events of the African slave trade and the New World plantation system. For Césaire, Negritude finds its meaning in the subjugation and exploitation experienced by the African peoples of the world. Through this common historical and cultural experience, the African people are bound together and "the compass of suffering" measures the richness of it. The fact that blacks have suffered collectively throughout modern history and culture is the glue that binds us together as a people, as a nation. With Césaire's counterpart, Senghor, Negritude represents the essence and core of unchanging African identity and black existence. Senghor's contribution did have a profound impact on value systems that had informed Western perceptions of blacks since the precolonial period.

In terms of language and its emphasis on African cultural identity, there is continuity with Asante's project. The language of Negritude in its profound literary expression is quite valuable to Asante's formulation of the Afrocentric perspective. Because Negritude lifted up the plight of suffering African peoples and affirmed the inherent value of being black, Asante indicates that writings such as these are liberating and essential to the Afrocentric outlook. Diop, on the other hand, finds the Negritude movement disconcerting when it suggests that blacks ought to embrace their emotional contribution to society alone. Diop argues that the Negritude poets lacked the scientific means to confront certain notions of black inferiority and accepted some of its views. Indeed, the contribution of the Negritude movement to the Afrocentric idea is profound. Although Asante borrows heavily from Diop in his historical argumentation, he parts company with Diop in his support of movements such as Negritude as it provides an alternative cultural literary perspective — a necessary dimension of the Afrocentric position.

Resisting Empire with the Pen: The Harlem Renaissance

The Harlem Renaissance is a historical event in African American history that has helped form our understanding of cultural identity as well as provided some precedence for the notion of Afrocentrism. Roberts writes, "The Harlem Renaissance was a brief but powerful period of black consciousness in artistic and literary modes of expression."[15] Unfolding during the 1920s and 1930s, the Harlem Renaissance was primarily a literary and intellectual movement involving a diversity of social and cultural expressions. Three essential literary works laid the foundation of what would become known as the "New Negro" movement. Claude McKay's volume of poetry, *Harlem Shadows* (1922), Jean Toomer with *Cane* (1923), and Jessie Fauset's *There Is Confusion* were major works that were published and recognized not only by the black literary community, but many whites had to take note as well. From this new literary fervor, organizations like the National Urban League, headed by Charles S. Johnson, came into being to aid these efforts. Through this mixture of intellectual and cultural expression a new revised sense of identity and self-determination was forged into the fabric of the black experience in America. Without question, the Harlem Renaissance has left an indelible mark upon the literary and intellectual landscape of African and African American arts and literature in the United States and abroad. The influences of the Harlem Renaissance have informed writers through history, from Ralph Ellison and Richard Wright of the 1930s and 1940s to Alice Walker and Toni Morrison of the 1980s and 1990s and beyond. In Asante's argument, there does appear to be some continuity with the Harlem Renaissance in terms of its reinterpretation of Africa as being the center of their cultural understanding. Asante recognizes the achievements of the Harlem Renaissance as seen in the witness of W. E. B. Du Bois. Du Bois prepared the world for Afrocentricity but was not Afrocentric himself. Nevertheless, the contributions of Du Bois and the Harlem Renaissance are indispensable to the Afrocentric outlook and what it means for us today.

Afrocentrism in the Postcolonial Context

After examining the historical record for precedence of the Afrocentric outlook and expression, let us now examine the positions of Asante and Diop in regard to Afrocentrism and the notion of cultural identity. The arguments of Asante and Diop are quite different — due in large measure to

15. J. Deotis Roberts, *Afrocentric Christianity: A Theological Appraisal for Ministry* (Valley Forge, Pa.: Judson, 2001), 22.

context, audience, and background. Diop was primarily aiming his writings at both the European and African scholarly community in order to prove that "Africa is the cradle of humanity." Asante is concerned with the "African cultural project" that advocates a new philosophical perspective that's ultimately guided by history and the shared experiences of African peoples. How are we to truly understand this intriguing movement known as Afrocentrism? What is its connection to the Christian church? Also, how does Diop's scientifically based argument aid in the quest for cultural identity and meaning for black people?

Another dimension of Afrocentrism is the notion of collective consciousness that's rooted in a shared historical cultural and intellectual history. An important part of this, Asante asserts, is the concept of Nija (the Way), and the "Teaching of Nija." Nija is the collective expression of the Afrocentric worldview grounded in the history of African people. Part of this formulation is the idea of collective consciousness. Before there can be unity, there must be collective consciousness, Asante asserts. Asante draws heavily on the experiences of Malcolm X and the black nationalist movement as an illustration of his position. According to Asante, Malcolm X recognized the necessity of having a shared consciousness among black peoples — a consciousness guided and perpetuated by the masses. A shared collective consciousness is what enables marginalized peoples of different backgrounds and contexts to band together, linking arms, in the struggle for freedom and justice. A postcolonial theology of liberation, fueled by a motif of prophetic rage, recovers the voices of figures like Malcolm X and Asante in a way that leads to a more fluid yet firm sense of cultural identity and community.

Community and Cultural Identity

Cultivating communities of resistance, rooted in a deep sense of shared identity, is essential to the task of liberation and casting alternative visions of the world. Developing a postcolonial theology of liberation means considering those alternative voices, like Cheikh Anta Diop, who called into question the presupposition of modernity as it related to African descendant peoples. Deemed one of the greatest scholars to emerge in the African world in the twentieth century, Diop was born in 1923 in Diourbel, Senegal, on the west coast of Africa, and rose to the heights of intellectual enterprise during the fervor of the Pan-Africanism movement, being led by America's

W. E. B. Du Bois, and the African independence explosion, beginning with Ghana in 1958. Diop creatively used the disciplines of linguistics, cultural and physical anthropology, history, chemistry, and physics that his research required. In doing so, Diop "forged new theoretical pathways and revealed new evidence in the quest to uncover the ancient origins and unifying principles of classical African civilization."[16] Some of the creative pathways into developing a sound conception for Africa as the "cradle of humanity" were illustrated in other important works by Diop. Among these were *Black Africa: The Economic and Cultural Basis for a Federated State* and the comprehensive work on African history, *The African Origin of Civilization: Myth or Reality*.[17] The former presented a blueprint for economic development in Africa through saving mineral wealth for unborn generations. This work was rarely read or understood. The latter is a one-volume translation of the major sections of two other books by Diop, *Nations nègres et Culture* and *Antériorité des civilisations nègres*. This work challenged historical and cultural presuppositions, particularly held among Western scholars, about the place and contribution of Africa in world history and intellectual discourse. By this challenge Diop changed the landscape and attitudes about the place of African people in history in scholarly circles around the world. The primary thrust of Diop's *African Origin of Civilization* is a redefinition of the place of Egypt in African history.

Out of this cultural and intellectual development came Diop's magnum opus, *Civilization or Barbarism: An Authentic Anthropology*. This is considered the last of Diop's great contributions to the clarification of African world history. It is in many regards a summation and an extension of his previous research; it is a refinement of his analyses and a final statement of his previous research, reflecting the completion of his mission. Diop stated before his death that this would be his last scholarly work, and indeed it was, as Diop left a political and social master plan that would save Africa for the Africans. For Diop, Africa is undoubtedly and unmistakably the "cradle of humanity," not merely at the *Homo erectus* stage (i.e., sapientization, from the adaptation of primitive African stock under geographical conditions), but also at the *Homo sapiens sapiens* stage. Africa is the birthplace of humanity. This fact has been deliberately falsified and

---

16. Cheikh Anta Diop, *The African Origin of Civilization: Myth or Reality*, trans. from the French by Mercer Cook (Chicago: Lawrence Hill Books, 1974), xiv.

17. Cheikh Anta Diop, *Civilization or Barbarism: An Authentic Anthropology*, trans. Yaa-Lengi Meema Ngemi (Brooklyn, N.Y.: Lawrence Hill Books, 1981).

manipulated by ill-intentioned Egyptologists like the French scholar Count Constantin de Volney, and other Western scholars.

Because Egypt is the "distant mother" of Western cultures and sciences, Diop maintains that these ideas are rooted in images of creation of African ancestors — seen in religious movements and thoughts like Judaism, Christianity, Islam, dialectics, the theory of being, the exact sciences, arithmetic, geometry, mechanical engineering, astronomy, medicine, literature (novel, poetry, drama), architecture, the arts, etc. Hence, the ideologies of Europe are not at all foreign to Africa. I find it truly insightful when Diop points out that no thought or philosophy can develop or be understood outside of its historical terrain. History, through anthropological and archaeological evidence, becomes the primary means to interpret and evaluate current strands of thought, whose place of origin Diop finds in classical Africa.

Diop engages the question of how to define "cultural identity" from three factors that contribute to its formation: history, language, and psychology. History and language are particularly emphasized in Diop's understanding of cultural identity. It is the history of a people that distinguishes them from merely a "population." The collective history is what connects a people to a shared past and thus renders a common destiny. Within history is a consciousness, a feeling of cohesion that provides security and a shield of cultural security for a people. Without this shared sense of history, there is nothing to connect them in action or consciousness. Historical continuity is perhaps the most viable weapon against outside aggression and disintegrating forces. Regardless of what that history might embody, what is important is the continuity of that history for the people who are a part of it. Diop proposes that the feeling of historical unity and cultural identity through scientific research is capable of contributing to the African cultural consciousness. This reinforces the cultural identity of the "Negro African peoples" throughout the world. Language serves as a constituent of cultural personality and of cultural identity. For Diop, the language of a people is the hope of a people. Within the rhythms of language is a common denominator for communicating cultural identity and consciousness. Like the European continent, there is ambiguity concerning African linguistic unity. Even though Africa has more than 360 languages and dialects, the African educational programs must be recast and the many African languages and dialects, some going back to Egypto-Nubian antiquity, must be centered, as is the Western educational system — having its foundation in Greco-Latin antiquity. This is possibly the most powerful and effective method of reinforcing African cultural personality and cultural identity among Africans and other peoples as well.

Lessons from Dark Waters:
Confronting the Problem of Identity and Nihilism

In American society, the question of cultural identity among African Americans continues to be problematic to the black community and broader society. Throughout history, African Americans have grappled with the issue of cultural identity. Roberts shares his own experience of the problem of self-definition. For instance, throughout the twentieth century, black people have been described as "colored," "Negro," "Afro-American," and in the most recent delineation, "African American." This vacillation of self-identification has had a profound impact on some of the most vulnerable members of our community, namely, black youth, who continue to search for meaning and identity. Roberts, in his visits to prisons, observed a tremendous lack of self-esteem among young black males. Many do not think highly of themselves and know little about their cultural heritage but are often led to believe they are of no value to the wider society and have a history replete with only slavery and oppression. What black youth must be taught is that their inherent worth comes from God because they are made in the image of God. Because of this, they have been created with a purpose and divine destiny. The task of the church is to let them know that because God loves them, we do too. This expression of love must be supported by uplifting their sense of dignity and self-worth. The Afrocentric idea, rooted in history and culture, has a powerful role in this task because it reminds youth that they are "somebody," that they are heirs to a rich and noble heritage and may walk with dignity and confidence because of it. Roberts sums up these sentiments: "Afrocentrism assures black youth that they come from a noble heritage. They need not be filled with self-hate. It is true that we were slaves and that the shadow of slavery still lingers in the form of discrimination. However, one can still affirm a sense of self-worth and move forward against all odds. By combining the Christian faith claim that we are made in the image of God with a sense of belonging to a noble race, we may be able to lift up our heads and aspire for a better and brighter future."[18]

18. Roberts, *Afrocentric Christianity*, 87.

The Afrocentric perspective might also play a significant role in economic and political developments. That Asante exposes a sense of shared consciousness means that we might somehow be able to work together to strengthen relations in the African American community and the wider society.

Conclusion

Forging a postcolonial theology of liberation, and lifting up the idea of prophetic rage as a creative motif in challenging empire and nihilism, is reinforced by the artistic and intellectual creativity of figures like Cullen, Du Bois, Diop, and Asante, who remind us of the beauty and brilliance of the black experience. They offer to us the resources that have helped to empower, sustain, project, and guide black lives through the treachery of colonialism, slavery, Jim Crow segregation, patriarchal systems, and poverty. Both Diop and Asante, in particular, provide exciting insights into how we understand the history and culture of Africa and its peoples. Diop adds to our understanding of cultural identity through his analysis of archaeological, anthropological, and scientific data, helping us to truly understand Africa's place in the development of human civilizations. Using the insights of Diop, Asante gives us an exciting new alternative for how to understand black identity as African descendant peoples. As Du Bois observed nearly a century ago, understanding the ways in which black peoples have survived and thrived, in spite of the corrosive forces of empire and nihilism, may very well provide the resources for cultures around the world to find meaning and hope as well.

CHAPTER SIX

No Ways Tired

I don't feel no ways tired,
I've come too far from where I started from.
Nobody told me that the road would be easy,
I don't believe He brought me this far to leave me.
I don't believe He brought me this far
I've been sick (I don't believe),
but God brought me (He brought me this far).
. . . I don't believe (I don't believe)
that God would bring me
(would bring me this far).
I don't believe (I don't believe)
that God would bring me
(would bring me this far).
I don't believe (I don't believe)
that God would bring me (would bring me this far just to
        leave me).

What is hope? When all appears to be lost, where does one find the will to fight, to resist, to hope, to trust, and the will to live? In the final analysis, there is no future without hope. It is hope that looks to the future, that exists in the future yet reaches back into the present to show what is possible and inevitable based on the will and way of God in the world. The world is crying out for hope. The nihilism that pervades the current predicament will not last. Nihilism is always conquered by hope with the refusal to die. For oppressed and marginalized communities, communities of suffering and fear, it is the will to fight and resist that nurtures and breeds hope like the sparks of an early flame dancing on a gentle breeze. In order to fight, hope must exist, and there is something about resistance itself that stirs up the power of hope.

The creative encounter between hope and resistance is exactly what must be urged today with a piercing sense of prophetic rage. As I discussed in the previous chapter, when black folks call upon their ancient God, the God of their ancestors, rooted in the cultural milieu of mother Africa, the resources for confronting present challenges emerge with resounding clarity. They interpreted and made sense of the God of Christianity as a God of liberation, hope, and reconciliation, a God that would break the bonds of slavery and oppression and deliver them into a future of promise, love, justice, and peace. The God of Jesus was looked upon as a God of both material and soul salvation, insomuch as God's liberating power was embodied and intelligible in the concrete, tangible act of human liberation from the throes of social and cultural, economic, and political systems that were hostile to black flourishing. In black theology, I see the hope and liberation of black folks intimately linked to the liberation and hope of all oppressed communities. None of us are free until all of us are free. None can truly speak unless all have the voice to speak. The binary frameworks of picking and choosing which forms of oppression are more legitimate and intense than others are no longer sufficient. Human suffering is multidimensional, fluid, and expansive. Thus, it requires an understanding of hope that is at once prophetic and imaginative, envisioning a God of radical love who cares as deeply for us as for our enemies. And the creative, passionate, and courageous task of bringing about liberation and hope, across boundaries, in concrete actions in this present world is but a glimpse of what is to come.

Prophetic Hope in the Shadows of Empire

Reclaiming the prophetic dimensions of the Christian heritage, and prophetic Christianity, in general, opens up vistas of promise and possibility for attending to empire and its companion nihilism. The idea of reclaiming the prophetic dimensions of the Christian heritage arises from the fact that God calls us to think and act in relation to all spheres of human experience — social, political, economic, and religious. What does it mean to be Christian in the context of social systems and structures that devalue and demean human life? My point of departure is the belief that because God is the God of all creation, there are no realms outside of or beyond God's redeeming love. Hope and justice as two dimensions of the same reality, reflected in the wells of the black experience in America and also resistance movements worldwide, open up numerous possibilities for creating and sustaining positive change. When hope is present, so are the foundations for creative responses to the crushing social conditions under which many blacks seem to be trapped. God's love is not passive but active and transformative. Through the reconciling work of God in Christ, Christians are called to be agents of reconciliation and social transformation, called to participate in what God is doing in the world.

I believe this question is further complicated by the critical questions illuminated in postmodern and postcolonial theological discourse, in that it deals with the cultural problem of nihilism, capitalistic desire, and the progressive allure of technology. Perhaps more prevalent among today's youth, the great ideas concerning social transformation or attempts at building a more hopeful and humane society seem nearly absent. This is due, in large measure, to the fact that many have lost confidence in the idea that one can actually change the world in which one lives. Those grand ideas are of little value in a technocratic and pluralistic age. I would agree with Gianni Vatimo, who observed that the notion of progress now comes under the disguise of technological advances. So with the development of every new smart phone or electronic gadget comes a perception of forward progression. But there is evidence to suggest that with all the technological progress, very little progress has been made when it comes to poverty, health care, the incarcerated, education, and the continuous onslaught of global war and nuclear proliferation. According to the World Health Organization (WHO), about 1.2 billion people now live in extreme poverty (living on an equivalent of less than a dollar a day). Millions are locked out of the economic process because they lack the capital necessary to participate in the current global market. What is at stake is a fair market system that values human life and is socially responsible, while at the same time providing the space for innovation and autonomy.

As we look out at the world today, it is very clear that the gift that is God's world is at its best troubled, and at its worst, in perilous crisis. The nihilistic threat has to do with the reality of hopelessness and despair, the death of a will to fight, giving up, refusing to live and let live. When there is an absence of meaning, of sense-making, when the grounding of our existence as human beings becomes fragile and the awareness of how God has created, ordered, and sustained the world is lost, life becomes devoid of form and substance. It becomes a maze of dull routine, reflecting the cadence of material gratification, yielding to what Daniel Bell calls those "technologies of desire."

The manufacturing of desire becomes the chief means of imprisoning bodies in the haze of nothingness and meaninglessness. The constant flood of information, infotainment, cell phones, iPads and iPods, digital technologies, music, etc., becomes a virtual prison of meaninglessness and nothingness meant to rob life of real meaning, hope, faith, and trust in God.

The prophetic dimensions of the Christian narrative that have spoken to realities of systemic evils, whether Gregory of Nyssa's call of the church to address the needs of power, Bonhoeffer's witness to the Third Reich in Germany, or Mother Teresa's prayers over the sick and dying at the Ganges River, are the sort of prophetic rage that can hold back the onslaught of suffering today. Prophetic rage is the courage to speak truth to power; to declare God's ways in the world; to challenge social systems and ground the reality of God's will in justice, freedom, and truth. It means challenging the persistent structures of imperialism, the prison-industrial complex, widespread poverty; and proclaiming that the same God who is Lord of the church is Lord over social systems and all areas of human life.

Prophetic rage is the call to remembrance; to remember the past, as living history in the present. A few years ago we celebrated the fiftieth anniversary of the Freedom Rides of 1961, where young black and white college students from across the country boarded buses to challenge the laws of segregation in the South. With their minds, bodies, and spirits, they called America to account for its social sins and broke the backbone of the demonic system of segregation in the South. Prophetic rage is right remembering in a way that claims the nakedness and brutality of the past for what it was — slavery, colonialism, segregation, apartheid, and other atrocities — recognizing that the same impulse to enslave, kill, and dominate lives on today. Times may change, but human nature remains constant. History allows us to gain a full picture of what it means to be human and what it means to challenge injustice and work for liberation in the world.

Prophetic rage is the call to resistance — to claim hope against hopelessness, meaning in the face of meaninglessness, faith where there is no faith, courage amid fear, joy in sadness, liberation in bondage. Prophetic rage is the call of a new generation to claim the authority of God's vicars of truth and justice in the world. It means remaining faithful, steadfast, unmovable, and firmly planted on truth, justice, and righteousness. "Let justice roll down like waters, and righteousness like a mighty stream."

Prophetic Courage in the Age of Obama

The election and reelection of President Barack Obama, amid the shadows of widening and deepening gaps between rich and poor across the nation and the world, represent a peculiar moment in history. On the one hand, the doors of opportunity appear to be more open than ever before. Obama's election in 2008 signaled a new chapter in the unfolding American theo-drama, representing almost a zeitgeist (or spirit of the times), as it relates to King's vision of his children one day living in a nation where they would be judged not by the color of their skin but by the content of their character. The signing of Obama's historic health-care legislation was certainly an expression of that hard-fought battle in the war of equality, freedom, and justice.

On the other hand, at the time of this writing, many are beginning to see that the demons of racism, materialism, militarism, and violence have ancient and virulent roots. Their meandering tentacles are as ancient and piercing as America itself. The black freedom struggle, steeped in the slave experience, born of freedom's songs and the feet of weary warriors of justice, serves as the fulcrum that makes American democracy intelligible and meaningful in the present moment and into the future. The freedom struggle and the desire of the enslaved and their children's children to be free, to live with dignity, justice, and in their full humanity — these values that America upholds in the Constitution are being challenged. The historic documents — the Constitution, Declaration of Independence, and the amendments to the Constitution — have been tried and tested through the passionate, prophetic, pensive, and persistent struggle to overcome racism, racialized violence, and political, economic, psychological, and social dehumanization.

Were it not for the bold and courageous pilgrimage of freedom fighters, both past and present, would we truly understand the words of the Declaration of Independence when it says, "We hold these truths to be self-evident, that all men are created equal, that they are endowed by their

Creator with certain unalienable Rights, that among these are Life, Liberty and the pursuit of Happiness"? While we must avoid any notions of valorizing or justifying the evils of slavery, lynching, American racism, and Jim Crow segregation, the fact is that the struggle for freedom, justice, and equality has helped America become what it is today, and remembering that struggle will dictate the future of the republic as well. Ralph Ellison, in his April 6, 1970, *Time* magazine essay "What America Would Be Like without Blacks," puts it this way:

> The fantasy of an America free of blacks is at least as old as the dream of creating a truly democratic society. While we are aware that there is something inescapably tragic about the cost of achieving our democratic ideals, we keep such tragic awareness segregated in the rear of our minds. We allow it to come to the fore only during moments of great national crisis. . . . The nation could not survive being deprived of their presence because, by the irony implicit in the dynamics of American democracy, they symbolize both its most stringent testing and the possibility of its greatest human freedom.

James Baldwin makes a similar observation, with artistic precision, as he makes a distinction between who he is and the ways in which American racialization has cast a certain identity upon him. In a crowded room of whites, Baldwin looks across the room and says with a kind of voracious and vigilant imagination, "If I am a nigga, you invented me." That is to say, the illusion and fiction of black inferiority and white supremacy served as stabilizing narratives in American cultural, political, and religious life, sustaining and perpetuating generations of racialized violence, economic disenfranchisement, and psychological and spiritual trauma. It was this struggle that Du Bois was referring to in *The Souls of Black Folks* (1903), as blacks are forced to vacillate in the wilderness of double-consciousness, between who they are (their true nature and being) and who they are compelled to be by virtue of the dominating systems of power and white supremacy at work in mainstream society.

The Emancipation Proclamation, as a war measure of Abraham Lincoln, which some historians say may have turned the tide during the Civil War in the Union's favor, was a major victory for the abolitionist movement. In it Lincoln proclaimed that "by virtue of the power and for the purpose aforesaid, I do order and declare that all persons held as slaves within said designated states and parts of states are, and henceforward shall be, free; and that the Executive Government of the United States, including the military and naval authorities thereof, will recognize and maintain the freedom of said persons."[1]

These words have resounded loudly over the last 150 years, all across the nation, from city to city, town to town, even in the small rural community of my own birth. I am not an immigrant. I am the descendant of the enslaved. Unlike President Obama, I grew up in the back hills of Georgia, on a dirt road at the edge of a former plantation. My great-great-grandfather was born in slavery. In a small house with seven sisters, a father who was a sanitation worker, and mother who was a nursing aide, I discovered life with an abysmal awareness of racialized systems of power meted out in the schools, local businesses, among law enforcement, the segregation of churches and communities, and in all dimensions of human life.

As early as seven years old, I spent most of my summers cropping long rows of tobacco in the sizzling heat. I looked on as white children experienced the wonders of summer camp and in-ground pools, where black children were put in positions where they had to work the fields, while others suffered, day to day, agonizing reminders of powerlessness, hopelessness, and, for some, lovelessness and lifelessness. And yet, through the unconquerable spirit of determination, they would gather in their Sunday finest, walk with dignified strides into houses of worship across the South, sing songs of hope, songs of freedom, songs of resilience, like "We've come this far by faith" and "Soon and very soon, we are going to see the King," with words like "time is filled with swift transition, naught of earth unmoved can stand, build your hopes on things eternal, hold to God's unchanging hand." Building on what Albert Raboteau called "slave religion," a religion steeped in perseverance, faith, hope, and love, I remember the proud full-bodied women adorned in lily-white dresses standing at the doors, as if awaiting a presidential appearance, moving with grace and dignity, as the preacher preached, as if enacting a great theatrical performance, with sweat dripping on aged Bibles, amid the frenzied motions of hands waving and bodies in motion like mist over an angry sea.

It was that beautiful chaos that shaped and formed the young Dr. King, that transformed a young Baptist preacher into a global visionary leader and revolutionary for all ages; that inspired leaders all over the world; and that captured the imagination of the young idealistic commu-

---

1. "Emancipation Proclamation," signed September 1862, and delivered January 1, 1863.

nity organizer by the name of Barack Hussein Obama, inspiring him to dream, sparking the slogan of millions with "Yes we can" and *Sí se puede.*

America is truly at a pivotal moment in human history. We are witnessing the browning and diversification of America and the planet, a fluidity of cultures, religions, races, ethnicities, bursting on the face of humanity like never before. Individuals and cultures from around the world are moving beyond their narrow enclaves and interrelating, sharing, talking, loving, living, and hoping together like never before.

The forces of technology, social networking, cyberspace, mass marketing, and mass communication, as well as the rise in transcontinental travel, now make possible the emergence of a global civilization, a world of differences, where long-held narratives such as white supremacy are being curtailed and disrupted, dismantled, and eulogized at the cemeteries of ideological history.

Yet the spirit of yesterday's sins still lingers. Poverty and social neglect have overtaken our world like a tidal wave. The problem of mass incarceration has created what Michelle Alexander calls a "new Jim Crow," and massive amounts of cultural violence have resulted in a rampage of social, political, and economic anxiety. We are facing not only fiscal cliffs, but also moral and spiritual cliffs. Now, on the fiftieth anniversary of the March on Washington and King's "I Have a Dream" speech, there is a more urgent need to reflect on the relationship between the black freedom struggle, President Obama (and subsequently his administration as well), and the legacy of Dr. King.

The fact is that Obama is not King and does not walk in the same trajectory. President Obama is now the face of empire. He is the commander in chief of the most powerful empire that the world has ever known. He was raised by his white grandparents and white mother with the Protestant ethic of Midwestern roots. The son of a Kenyan, Obama knew very little of his father and the African world. His mother imported black culture to him as a child and encouraged him to ground his identity in the songs of freedom and the black freedom struggle. He listened to jazz and blues, the spirituals, and speeches by Dr. King and Malcolm X. He observed his activist mother fighting for the rights of the poor and marginalized in the streets of Indonesia and Hawaii. Obama also entered the ranks of the elite as a student at Columbia University, and later as a law student at the prestigious Harvard Law School, where he became editor of the revered *Harvard Law Review.*

King, on the other hand, was too a descendant of the enslaved.

Through generational memory and experience, King was handed down a tradition of racial struggle and the quest for freedom. He was heir to three generations of black Baptist preachers. He too would become a Baptist preacher, yet steeped in the field of Boston personalism. Freedom, justice, human dignity, and nonviolence would be his thunderous cries. These cries were heard in these words on the steps of the Lincoln Memorial amid the sweltering heat of an August afternoon in 1963: "I have a dream that the sons of former slaves and the sons of former slave owners . . . will be able to join hands and sing in the words of the old Negro spiritual, 'Free at last! free at last! thank God Almighty, we are free at last!'" These words were not simply utterances of a disheveled, insignificant preacher from Sweet Auburn Street in Atlanta, Georgia. They were indeed the sounds of prophetic illumination that may well determine the destiny of humanity. For these words and the movement they inspired summon that courageous trumpet of community amid difference, the hope for a world without violence or the need for violence, a world of dignity and respect for difference, of love and compassion for neighbor, a world free of poverty and need, where people can be all that God has created them to be. In the speech, King spoke of a bad check that America had issued to its African descendant peoples, a check that "has come back marked insufficient funds." He spoke of America living up to its creed and overcoming the voices of those mouths in the South dripping with the "words of interposition and nullification." And yet, he still urged us to dream on a little longer until justice becomes a reality and freedom rings from "every hill and molehill of Mississippi," and "from every mountainside," that it should ring resoundingly until "justice rolls down like waters, and righteousness like a mighty stream."

Indeed, those bells rang out as President Obama was sworn in for yet another term as anxious and excited supporters and well-wishers flocked to the capital city to catch a glimpse of history unfolding before their very eyes. Amid the gaze of history upon us, there are still tasks before us, particularly during these great moments of remembrance, celebration, and hope. Some of those tasks, left undone by history's sorrow, require that we insist on a radical revisitation of the past and that we remember rightly! The memory of the past will not go away. It must neither degenerate into mythology nor serve as an occasion for hatred and strife. It must be revisited as a source of hope and resilience in working toward a better day and a better world.

Now is the time to build multiracial, multiethnic, and multireligious coalitions, to establish dangerous alliances of justice, peace, nonviolence, and reconciliation that will leave a legacy to our children's children, a legacy steeped in coalitions of mutual cooperation and transformation. We must reclaim the tradition of radical orthopraxis, where there is a wedding of ideas and action, where theory and praxis merge. That would mean overcoming the blind spots of the modern era, a movement that tended to separate thought from actions, perhaps even head from heart. Reclaiming this tradition, a tradition of the spirituals and freedom songs, of marches and radical love, of hope and dignity, will pave the way for others in ways that we could never imagine. It may well help build an expansive, inclusive vision of global justice and difference, where silenced voices speak, the weak are empowered, and the blind are enlightened.

Conclusion

In his wonderful little book of reflections, entitled *God Has a Dream*, Desmond Tutu describes walking through the garden on the grounds of his home in Cape Town just at the turn of spring. Tutu's description of the transfiguration is a fitting illustration of both the call of the prophetic and the hope that resides in the redeeming work of God in Christ. He saw an image that was covered in snow, yet slowly, as the light of day broke through, the snow began to melt away, revealing an image of Jesus. For Tutu, it was an illustration of the transfiguration as the light revealed the true nature of a statue, and an image of what is to come.

With the magnitude of suffering that continues to exist in the world today, it seems particularly challenging to experience God's glory and divine presence in the world. We have seen unimaginable disasters in recent years, at home with Hurricane Katrina and the earthquake in Haiti, and abroad with the raging dogs of war in Iraq and now its intensification in Afghanistan. The disparity between rich and poor seems to be growing like never before — where 80 percent of the world's resources are absorbed by 20 percent of its population, primarily in the West, while much of the rest of the world (80 percent of its population) are forced to live off of the other meager 20 percent. It was recently reported that before the earthquake in Haiti, most people in the country lived off of less than twenty cents a day; this is similar to the many in the developing world who are challenged to live on less than a dollar a day.

When we think of the rising cost of health care, massive unemployment, and the housing shortage in many neighborhoods and communities around the country, most of us sit with agonizing frustration, shadows of despair, and dark clouds of fear and worry. The image of the transfiguration is particularly significant in these times of suffering, frustration, fear, and unrequited anxiety. The transfiguration of Moses in the Exodus narrative and of Jesus in Luke's Gospel serve as a glimpse of the kingdom of God in power coming into being. They invite the reader into a riveting saga of the mystery of God's reign over all life and reality, and how God's power and glory change and transform human life.

Moses, perhaps the greatest prophet, was transfigured at the top of Mount Sinai with a transformative encounter with God. It was, in fact, the glory of God, the presence of God, that transfigured Moses' entire being. The transfiguration of Moses' face served as confirmation that the law (the very means by which God comes to establish God's way of being in the world) comes from God, the light and life-giver; from God the liberator, who comes to establish God's reign of justice, peace, community, and interdependence on God and neighbor. The text says Moses' skin began to transform as he talked with God. God's light or the Shekinah (divine presence of God) engulfed the prophet. Moses' experience is the shadow of what was to come in the person of Jesus, who walks in the prophet tradition as liberator, arbiter of God's love and justice in the world.

Jesus' transfiguration, like Moses', served as confirmation of his Sonship and divine authority; that Jesus is at once prophet, priest, and king as the bearer of God's glory in human life. Some say that Jesus, who was praying at the time, was so drawn into the mystery of God's divine presence that the very unfathomable and incomprehensible power of the life of God overtook him. In perhaps one of the most dramatic passages in the New Testament, written by the meticulous hand of Saint Luke, we find the story of this mountain experience of Jesus. This was a mountain experience like no other. Frequently he would go up to the mountain to pray and return refreshed, renewed, revived, and reinvigorated by the Spirit of God and endowed with power from on high.

A week earlier, Jesus had a conversation with his disciples and said to Peter, "Who do the people say that I am?" Peter said, "Some say John the Baptist, others say Elijah or one of the prophets has risen." About this time, the people really didn't know who Jesus was. All they knew was that there was power in this man Jesus; that there were healing and forgiveness, and joy and mercy and love and compassion, in this man Jesus of Nazareth. Then Jesus said to Peter, "Peter, what about you, who do you say that I am?" and Peter said, "Thou art the Christ, Son of the living God!" There was no disputing the fact that there was power in the person of Jesus; that there were healing, transformation, renewal, and empowerment as Jesus embodied the power and wisdom of God in the world. The word was spreading about Jesus, and it seems as if Luke was portraying a kind of growing intensity, and urgency of discipleship and trust in Jesus' words and life. You hear it in these earlier words: "If any man will come after me, let him deny himself, take up his cross daily and follow me! For whosoever will save his life shall lose it and whosoever will lose his life for my sake, the same shall save it!"

He took Peter, James, and John up into the mountain to pray. The fashion of his countenance was altered, and his raiment was white and glistering. And standing there with him in glory were two of the greatest figures in the history of Israel — that great deliverer Moses and that towering prophet Elijah.

It is this vision, both of Moses and of Jesus, that confirmed the ways in which God's mystery, power, and glory were at work in their lives. Now, of course, the modern eye is quite suspicious of the mysterious and the miraculous. In our amazingly technological culture, we live in a world where real and fantasy have converged, where the miraculous is cast as the realm of the "magical" unreal world of make-believe and the imagined. Blockbuster movies like *Avatar, The Matrix, Lord of the Rings,* and television fare like *Hero, Lost,* and other programs, depict a world where fantasy and reality are merged. Even infotainment and the sensationalism of cable news networks like CNN, Fox News, MSNBC, and others project a world constantly on the brink of disaster, rigidly divided, ripped with conflict and turmoil; a world suspicious of the unexplainable, or doubting that massive transformative change is even possible in our time.

Yet, the image of the transfiguration for Moses and Jesus still offers a resounding message in our own time that the glory and power of God have the capacity to change our lives and our world through creative encounters in God. Many nuances can be drawn from these images of the transfiguration. First, an encounter with God has the capacity to change, transform, renew, reform, and transfigure reality. There is something quite mysterious about the way God's presence — the power, wisdom, incomprehensible fullness of God — changes us, captivates, quickens, and perhaps even disturbs our way of being, the very essence of who we are. Through us, God also transfigures our world by giving us the ability to imagine new possibilities, promises, gifts, ideas, and ways of being (even ordering our individual and communal lives, social institutions, churches, and the public square).

In 1989, no one could have imagined that apartheid as a legalized system of segregation and political subjugation would soon be a thing of the past in the Republic of South Africa. Yet, with the release of Nelson Mandela after twenty-seven years in a lonely jail cell on desolate Robben Island, apartheid not only came to an end, but South Africans also witnessed the election of their first black president. Of course, the nation struggles with racial and economic equality as the lingering legacy of apartheid is still present, but the transformation of the new, free South Africa still offers a glimpse of what is possible and what human beings, when open to the prophetic imagination and illumination of God's divine presence, can experience together.

The same could be said about the election of America's first black president. It signals on the one hand that great progress has been made in the quest for freedom, justice, and equality, that King's hope of his children one day living in a nation where people would be judged not by the color of their skin but by the content of their character might be a step closer. In the current political climate, amid the fierce debates over health care, the economy, and unemployment, it is difficult to imagine that in the election of 2008 the nation witnessed one of the greatest multicultural, inclusive, and energetic elections in the history of the American democratic process. People (young and old, black and white, Latino and Asian, rich and poor) who had never participated in the democratic electoral process before got involved. The election invited a renewed sense of agency in the capacity of ordinary people to enact change and transformation. I believe the election had less to do with Barack Obama (the individual) than it did with the deep, profound desire of many to envision some greater, more hopeful reality, which comes to mind at the thought of Obama's election. While there is still much work to do in advancing race relations in America (from segregated residential neighborhoods to segregated pews; economic disparities and political differences), it serves as a historical illustration of what is possible when we use our prophetic imaginations and attempt to understand our lives in light of God's glory and presence.

These experiences, of Mandela's or Obama's election, or of King's March on Washington, or of the miracle of large and small triumphs on a daily basis, give us insight into God's power of transformation and transfiguration in our lives and in the world. For Jesus and the disciples, as with Moses and his followers, the transfiguration was confirmation that they had divine companionship in their quest to live out God's way of being in the world. The text says that as Jesus prayed, the fashion of his countenance was altered. As he prayed, his clothes became white and glistening. As he prayed, I'm sure the scars he had attained through his earthly journey were no longer there; his fatigue from the long journey up the mountain had disappeared. And there standing before him in glory were Moses and Elijah. No doubt for Jesus this was a consoling experience. This was an uplifting experience. This tells us that while we are on the journey of life, we need consolation. Every now and then we need a word of encouragement, and when we go to the Lord and are in the presence of God's people, we receive the consolation we need.

The plight of marginalized and oppressed peoples of the world might be expressed in a familiar African American song: "I'm coming up on the rough side of the mountain; I'm doing my best to make it in!" "Like a ship that's toss'd and driven; Battered by an angry sea; When the storms of life are raging and their fury falls on me, I wonder what I have done that makes this race so hard to run; then I say to my soul, take courage; the Lord will make a way somehow!"

The great mystic theologian Howard Thurman said that we must always encounter God with both head and heart, that bringing to God all of who we are is where God meets us and transforms us, perhaps even transfigures us into new beings for God's glory and love. Thurman was echoing the familiar phrase of Pascal, who once observed that "the heart has reasons the mind cannot comprehend." Inviting the creative resources of God's power — love, justice, truth, and joy of God in our lives — enables us to overcome the challenges before us and those greater challenges that press against God's ways in the world.

James Weldon Johnson spoke to this when he wrote, "God of our weary years; God of our silent tears; thou who has brought us thus far along the way; thou who has by thy might led us into the light, keep us forever in thy path, we pray."[2] In the face of the unexplainable, the impulse is to respond with fear, incredulity, doubt, or idolatry. Fear, because there is a deep human desire to understand and explain how we experience the world; when circumstances or experiences arise that cannot be accounted for based on our view of the world, fear can be a very powerful and pervasive force in embedding the transformative power of God's divine presence.

This can be seen especially in terms of justice issues or whenever

2. James Weldon Johnson, "Lift Every Voice and Sing" (1900).

fresh perspectives are introduced that challenge, perhaps, our particular viewpoints. It is comforting to remain in the space of the known world, the familiar; to set up camp in those spaces (ways of being, thinking, acting, loving, living, etc.), because they reaffirm our deeply held perceptions, attitudes, beliefs, and general understandings about the world. They also reinforce certain normative practices; our lived experiences can have an extremely compelling influence on how we think and act, what we hold dear, and the critical questions we take up on a daily basis.

Think about the radical differences in the early Christian experience within the context of slavery in America. On the one hand, it was a dynamic moment in American religious life when the British Puritan traditions gave rise to an exciting multitude of dynamic faith communities — from Baptists to Methodists, Episcopalians, Presbyterians, as well as the Anabaptist tradition with Mennonites, Quakers, Shakers, and others. On the other hand, it was also one of the most painful and tragic eras in American history, which also gave rise to what Albert Raboteau called the "invisible institution" or the beginnings of the "black church" in America. During this era, as in our own time, there were competing visions for what constitutes the glory and presence of God. Is the presence of God experienced in the flourishing of one group at the expense of another; or liberation of the enslaved, downtrodden, poor, or marginal voices of the land? How do we begin to understand what it means to experience God's divine presence with an awareness of our own fragility and self-interest?

In the global world, images of the transfiguration as prophetic illumination enable us to continue to be open to new ideas, cultures, methodologies, theological perspectives, and narratives. If God is the God of all creation — all cultures, languages, communities, and individuals around the world and throughout the cosmos — then recognizing the ways in which God's divine presence is at work throughout creation means that difference is a gift of creation. The fellowship of Jesus with Moses and Elijah witnessed in the transfiguration was confirmation that Jesus was part of a larger kinship in the life of God, both past and present. It was a recognition, in many ways, that God calls us into community with others. The transfiguration brings us into an awareness of the divine companionship and friendship we have in God and those on a similar journey to experience the richness and fullness of God's presence as well.

When we remain open to be transfigured by God's divine glory with prophetic rage — remaining open to change, transformation, renewal, and prophetic illumination in the unfathomable wisdom and mystery of God

— we open ourselves up to amazing possibilities in the life of God. God's prophetic illumination makes known the unknown, illuminates and lights those shadowy crevices of our lives, challenging our understandings, exposing our blind spots, brightening our imaginations. When the disciples who were asleep awakened to the sight of Jesus, Moses, and Elijah standing in glory, they were astonished and wanted to pitch a tent; they wanted to stay there and savor the moment. I'm sure the disciples felt it couldn't get any better than that. And oftentimes, in the wake of great encounters and experiences, the temptation is to want to remain in that space of comfort and ecstasy, but there is much more work to be done. The transfiguration was also meant to inspire, encourage, and renew and embolden human lives, as a source of strength to continue the great work that needed to be done.

Perhaps we will find the courage to be persistent and find a renewed sense of determination to live out God's call for justice, peace, healing, and restoration in the world. Or perhaps we will find the quiet courage to face the challenges and burdens of our everyday lives, to maneuver through the complex web of momentary decision making, to live with integrity and humility; with love and respect for our neighbor; to walk with freedom and human dignity in all areas of our lives. Harriet Du Autermont said it best: "No vision and you perish, No ideal and you're lost; Your heart must ever cherish some faith at any cost. Some hope, some dream to cling to, some rainbow in the sky, some melody to sing to, some service that is high!"[3] There is a familiar song that even in all its simplicity speaks to each of us in resounding ways:

> This little light of mine
> I'm gonna let it shine
> Let it shine, let it shine, let it shine!

---

3. Harriet Du Autermont, "No Vision and You Perish" (New York: Doubleday, 1994).

CHAPTER SEVEN

Building the World House

The whole history of progress of human liberty
Shows that all concessions
Yet made to her august claims
Have been born of earnest struggle.
If there is no struggle
There is no progress.
Those who profess to favor freedom,
And yet deprecate agitation,
Are men [and women] who want crops
Without plowing up the ground,
They want rain
Without the awful roar of its waters.[1]

We have inherited a large house, a great "world house" in which
we have to live together — black and white, Easterner and West-
erner, Gentile and Jew, Catholic and Protestant, Moslem and
Hindu — a family unduly separated in ideas, culture and inter-
est, who, because we can never again live apart, must learn some-
how to live with each other in peace.[2]

---

1. Frederick Douglass, "No Struggle, No Progress," 1857.
2. Martin Luther King Jr., *Where Do We Go from Here: Chaos or Community?* (reprint, Eugene, Oreg.: Wipf and Stock, 2002), 195.

If prophetic rage is nothing else, it is the merging of thought and action as one continual process, and refusal to cease hoping, resisting, fighting, praying, and striving. Action gives way to thought and thought fuels progressive action. Forging a progressive social agenda and building what Martin Luther King Jr. described as the "world house" mean establishing a progressive agenda that is at once strategic and fluid, open to flow and movement, always changing and adapting. The present moment calls for a progressive social agenda, moving beyond reactionary, knee-jerk, temporary responses to the complex and difficult issues confronting marginalized and oppressed communities the world over. Domestic issues, including reforming immigration, dealing with mass incarceration, reforming America's schools, and procuring a living wage for all Americans, remain among the most urgent social concerns of our time. Internationally as well as domestically, the plague of poverty continues to be the most corrosive and pervasive force of suffering in our world. In resisting and overcoming these challenges, a progressive agenda must take into account the comprehensive dynamics of social, political, economic, spiritual, and religious forces involved in the creation of flourishing black communities. Additionally, as a black theologian, I am concerned about empowering and uplifting the black community, and as a postcolonial theologian of liberation, I am concerned with building a public vision that affirms the flourishing of all God's children as well. Our destinies are intertwined.

This comprehensive justice agenda will ensure that we care for all God's children. As Dr. King said in the "Letter from Birmingham Jail," "Injustice anywhere is a threat to justice everywhere." Whenever we see injustice in our world, in any form, we need to be vigilant in mobilizing citizen-activists to work for justice in local communities, connected by related national and global movements. This comprehensive justice agenda offers all Americans, in particular, a constructive way to transform our prophetic rage into positive, constructive programs and policies that can build the beloved community in our cities, states, and nation. The notion that, through a comprehensive justice agenda, we can make the world better and live into the beloved community is not utopian. It can and will occur as individuals and communities translate their prophetic rage into creative, sustained, and shared engagements with local, national, and global programs and policies.

Here, we are invited to share in the prophetic legacy of Dr. King, who once observed that "we have inherited a great house, a world house . . .

where we must learn to live together as brothers or perish as fools."[3] Only by engaging in a direct effort to change public policy, as well as lift up the salvation of Jesus Christ to change the hearts, minds, and bodies of individuals, can we begin to shift the paradigm of suffering and hopelessness in many of our communities nationwide. What we stand in need of is "a vision of God's own cleanup of God's own world now grown toxic from evil and impurity, injustice and oppression, war and violence."[4]

A World House: Thinking Globally, Acting Locally

Prior to his assassination in Memphis, Tennessee, Martin Luther King Jr. and freedom fighters from around the nation were engaged in the Poor People's Campaign. The campaign called for a "bill of rights for the poor." It was recognition of the interrelatedness of the issues and challenges of the poor and the anxiety of the middle class. The campaign, for King, signaled the emergence of a new global economy, one based on human dignity and freedom. King vehemently believed that by transforming the economic system in America — given America's role as the chief engine of the global economy — the campaign could very well bring an end to poverty and social instability among developing nations. He believed that the Poor People's Campaign could change America from within, and change the world as an inevitable outcome. In King's mind, changing America meant changing the world. By redirecting America's imperial powers from domination and violence to compassion and good will for all, it would be possible to create new ways of engaging in statecraft and conceptions of political power. "What is needed is a realization that power without love is reckless and abusive, and love without power is sentimental and anemic. Power at its best is love implementing the demands of justice, and justice at its best is power correcting everything that stands against love."[5]

King's critique of the war in Vietnam examined the ways in which the state could use power either to benefit humanity or to corrode the very

---

3. King, *Where Do We Go?* 194.

4. John Dominic Crossan, *God and Empire: Jesus against Rome, Then and Now* (New York: HarperSanFrancisco, 2007), 82.

5. King, *Where Do We Go?*; also in James Melvin Washington, ed., *A Testament of Hope: The Essential Writings of Martin Luther King, Jr.* (New York: Harper and Row, 1986), 245.

core of the body politic. King was able to make theological and ethical connections with civil religion, war, and poverty. He surmised that the massive amount of resources being spent on wars and militarism around the world could be used to alleviate poverty. Even now, there is a growing awareness that the source of terrorism and many militaristic threats to U.S. interests comes down to poverty and economic disparities. He saw war as a vortex of the common good, sucking the very life out of the soul of community and a cultural sense of mutuality. "Now, it should be incandescently clear that no one who has any concern for the integrity and life of America today can ignore the present war. If America's soul becomes totally poisoned, part of the autopsy must read 'Vietnam.' It can never be saved so long as it destroys the deepest hopes of men [and women] the world over. So it is that those of us who are yet determined that 'America will be' are led down the path of protest and dissent, working for the health of our land."[6]

King's vision of the world house reflected an understanding of the interconnectedness and interrelatedness of individuals, cultures, faiths, races, ethnicities, classes, genders, and nations around the world. King could have never fathomed the great advances made in social networking, global trade, mass communication, and digital technology that connect and reconnect human beings as never before in human history. The world house, rooted in his notion of the beloved community, provides an expansive and inclusive vision of justice and differences. It provides a way of imagining a world where differences are celebrated and not negated. King's global vision of the world house was inspired by not only his work in cities like Montgomery, Selma, Albany, and Memphis, but also his exchange with global leaders and his gaze beyond American shores. King was in dialogue with African leaders like Kwame Nkrumah (anticolonialist, first president of an independent Ghanaian state) and Albert Luthuli (president of the African National Congress from 1952 to 1967, South Africa). King wrote,

> If we look honestly at the realities of our national life, it is clear that we are not marching forward; we are groping and stumbling; we are divided and confused. Our moral values and our spiritual confidence sink, even as our material wealth ascends. In these trying circum-

6. Martin Luther King Jr., "Beyond Vietnam: A Time to Break the Silence" (speech delivered at Riverside Church, New York City, April 4, 1967).

stances, the black revolution is much more than a struggle for the rights of Negroes. It is forcing America to face all its interrelated flaws — racism, poverty, militarism, and materialism. It is exposing evils that are rooted deeply in the whole structure of our society. It reveals systemic rather than superficial flaws and suggests that radical reconstruction of society itself is the real issue to be faced.[7]

King anticipated the postmodern dilemma — prominence of technological advances; expanding multinational corporations; decentering of Europe as base of world power and hegemonic influence; intensification of American imperialism and militarism; and instability, crisis, and change. We have dramatically moved from the problem of "production" to the problem of "consumption." It has become a reversal of Paul's dictum ("anyone unwilling to work should not eat" [2 Thess. 3:10]), to the notion that if people will not eat (and drink and buy compact discs and travel, and buy the latest fashions, appliances, etc.) in sufficient volume, then no one will work.[8] Michael Budde's *The (Magic) Kingdom of God: Christianity and Global Culture Industries* offers a poignant assessment of these new global realities. There are shifts in political focus and civil rights focus toward the problem of poverty; entrenched social, political, and religious commitment to the "status quo" and maintenance of established power; persistent economic inequities due to racial discrimination; and racial bias that continues to inform local, domestic, and foreign policy.

> The hard cold facts today indicate that the hope of the people of color in the world may well rest on the American Negro and his ability to reform the structure of racial imperialism from within and thereby turn the technology and wealth of the West to the task of liberating the world from want.[9]

> The poor can stop being poor if the rich are willing to become even richer at a slower rate.[10]

---

7. King, in Washington, *A Testament of Hope*, 313.

8. See Michael Budde, *The (Magic) Kingdom of God: Christianity and Global Culture Industries* (Boulder, Colo.: Westview, 1997).

9. King, *Where Do We Go?* 66.

10. Martin Luther King Jr., quoting Hyman Bookbinder, assistant director of the Office of Economic Opportunity, December 29, 1966.

Building the world house vision means establishing links between the domestic racial struggle for freedom and global injustices in Asia, South Africa, and Latin America. It also means attending to the issue of poverty on an international scale, bridging the gulf between scientific and moral progress and establishing a meaningful global ethic grounded in human dignity and freedom for all. It involves embracing an understanding of mutual global dependency. "We are everlasting debtors to known and unknown men and women. When we arise in the morning, we go into the bathroom where we reach for a sponge, which is provided for us by a Pacific islander. We reach for soap that is created for us by a European. Then at the table we drink coffee, which is provided for us by a South American, or tea by a Chinese or cocoa by a West African. Before we leave for our jobs we are already beholden to more than half of the world."[11]

Now in the age of Obama, the nation and the world still struggle with poverty as never before. Poverty simply exposes deeper challenges related to cultural, gender, religious, racial, and ethnic differences. So there is a persistent need to cast a prophetic vision of inclusivity and justice, which is expansive, to make room for unheard voices and the fluid nature of marginality as well. Here, the beloved community serves as a continual image of expansive/inclusive justice and community. Prophetic Christianity offers a radical critique of American politics and culture and a response to nihilism.

Prophetic Rage as Creative Love in Action

I am convinced now more than ever before that radical love matched with prophetic protest must become the central response of all who seek to make the world a better place. The intellectual and activist, politician and preacher, banker and borrower alike, must engage in the kind of passionate and self-sacrificial response to nihilism and human suffering that has characterized moments of social crisis throughout history. Ideas do not always lead to creative action or praxis. There is a creative relationship between praxis and *orthos*. They are intertwined.

Nearly fifty years after the March on Washington, the quest for justice, freedom, and human dignity continues. Yet, now, that great dream that Dr. King bled and died for is perilously close to being lost. Assaults on

11. King, *Where Do We Go?* 211.

the marginalized and poor are being waged from all sides, from the disenfranchisement of voters, to unemployment, mass incarceration, apartheid-like immigration laws, unlawful detention and detainment, police brutality, growing disparities in education, and the raging beast of militarism. The current conditions facing workers, poor African Americans and Latino/Latina Americans, have gone well beyond crisis mode and have reached the agonizing depths of human rights violations. The very legitimacy and validity of the criminal justice system, many social service agents, and perhaps even state legislatures, especially across Southern and Midwestern states, are being called into question.

Now is the time for workers, African Americans, Latino/Latina Americans, Euro-Americans, Asian Americans, and others, to recognize our common struggle, a struggle that reaches back to the very foundations of our democracy, a struggle that was championed by Dr. King and others who stood for justice and dignity for the powerless of our society. Events related to the Trayvon Martin shooting expose the depth of the struggle and the prophetic rage circulating through the veins of American society. The case is simply a symbol and embodiment of some of the greatest problems in American society. This event has provoked the need to introduce a broad, multidimensional coalition that makes connections in a common struggle for justice, equality, and human dignity for all people. All around the country today people are calling on their states to engage in massive social reform. There is a new awakening and awareness that we are all in this together, that if one part of the boat is sinking, it won't be long before the entire boat goes under. So it behooves us all to seal the hole, fix the boat, and start sailing!

The present moment demands that we work harder than ever before, walk together like never before, and struggle like never before, recognizing that the problems we face are interconnected and interrelated, from establishing a living wage and benefits for workers, to reforming health care for children and families, to ending mass incarceration in America, to enacting just and humane immigration reform, to curtailing the iron feet of militarism abroad, to reforming education, and to changing Wall Street and the fundamental economic structures in a way that serves the interest of working families.

We must restore justice and humanity to American society, in our local communities, where we affirm the inherent dignity and value of all human life, and affirm that as a society we will not tolerate human beings living in conditions less than what God has intended in God's world. We must restore justice and humanity to our economic system and affirm the voices of friends in the Occupy movement who speak for the 99 percent of Americans who have been pushed off the great island of prosperity and wealth, left to fend for themselves in the great ocean of poverty and unemployment. We must restore justice and humanity to an educational system that leaves millions of children without access to quality education and resources, and ensure decent wages for teachers across the board. We must put justice and humanity back into our criminal justice system.

We must recognize the connections between mass incarceration, which has become a means of social control among poor and marginalized communities, and immigration reform. The African American community and the Latino community have taken the brunt of unjust police profiling, mass incarceration, and unlawful detention, devastating families and communities across the nation. The same economic and political forces that have impacted the Latino community, such as NAFTA and unjust policies of globalization, have impacted poor African American communities as black folks struggle for jobs in the inner city. William Julius Wilson, the noted sociologist, has written well about the relationship between unemployment and poverty, and the conditions in the black community that lead to corroding economic conditions, from housing to unemployment, incarceration, and education.

A growing temptation and disturbing trend in many churches today is acquiescence to capitalistic desire and an uncritical obsession with what Nicholas Wolterstorff calls "victorious living" ideologies. By prophetic, I mean seriously considering and responding to the systemic forces at work in the lives of the poor. Resistance requires curtailing the lure of capitalistic desire. Daniel Bell offers an instructive approach as he draws a distinction between those "technologies of desire" created by the massive economic marketing machinery of Madison Avenue and the like, and the "disciplines of desire" displayed in the biblical call to self-denial and living for the other.

The Agenda

The model and experience of activism in the black church serve as a great illustration in building communities of resistance and action. A recent book, *The Covenant with Black America*, by Tavis Smiley, called together leading voices from across the country and outlined a provocative proposal for developing a progressive social agenda. The book, however, did not address the unique contributions and role of progressive and prophetic religious leaders within and beyond the black church in establishing change. For instance, black churches in particular are in the trenches, in the crucible of suffering in our communities. The black church still holds the moral authority for shaping the lives of black folks across the country. Indeed, it is still the black preacher that African Americans look to for spiritual guidance, constructive vision, and passionate leadership on issues of social justice, healing, and political action.

The black church, and its friends in other faith communities, has the grand opportunity of advancing these efforts through the mighty army of God's people who are also citizens of these United States of America. The statistics for the discussion below are daunting, and I won't revisit them here. Below is a synopsis of what can be done among policy makers to improve this area. That does not mean that personal responsibility is not essential. Many of our leaders have always and are continuing to call for responsible personal behavior. However, forging an urban agenda for the African American community means holding public leaders accountable and pushing forward some of the following initiatives.

Mass Incarceration: Where Empire and Local Communities Collide

An overwhelming chorus of voices from both within the corrections system and among politicians and community activists is calling for radical change from current jailing/corrections policies. Many are now becoming painfully aware that the present system is not working. Simply incarcerating individuals for lengthy sentences is not effective as a deterrent and does not contribute to a reduction in crime. Many of the current policies and practices that reflect strict sentencing policies and no-holds-barred policing and incarceration were fueled by late-1980s-and-1990s politically motivated "Get Tough on Crime" and "War on Drugs" programs.[12]

The dramatic shift from rehabilitation to retribution as a paradigm for addressing criminality and jailing/corrections developed largely out of

12. Andrew Black, "'The War on People': Reframing 'The War on Drugs' by Addressing Racism within American Drug Policy through Restorative Justice and Community Collaboration," *University of Louisville Law Review* 46 (Fall 2007): 179-99.

the desire of politicians to use public fear as a campaign platform for election, and also the sensationalism of television and media in covering violent crimes. A common slogan in newsrooms is "If it bleeds, it leads." To increase and sustain ratings, television and media often intensify public fears and anxieties, especially among suburbanites, despite the reality that most crimes occur in the community where individual offenders live. This means that in the city of Louisville, because of the highly segregated nature of the West Louisville community (predominately African American), most of the arrests occur among neighbors, friends, relatives, and fellow community members.

The problem with the current system is that it does not address the ravaging of communities when individuals (fathers, brothers, mothers, sisters, uncles, etc.) are removed for long periods of unproductive time. The present system also does not address the more complex system issues of poverty, unemployment, housing, the cultural particularities related to mentoring, social and religious life, and the nearly 70 percent of single-female-led households. William Julius Wilson, in his groundbreaking book *When Work Disappears,* makes a compelling case for the connection between poverty in the urban setting and high levels of arrest and subsequent incarceration. According to Wilson, it is dangerous and socially/economically irresponsible to continue to incarcerate individuals without looking at the searing problems of poverty that continue to plague the African American community. By investing in the development and economic foundations of predominately poor African American males, says Wilson, we will not only ensure public safety but also contribute to a vibrant and flourishing community for all.

Political scientists, sociologists, and criminologists are not the only ones concerned with the corrections systems. The criminal justice and corrections systems, as a function of the public good, impact all aspects of the community. Social and religious leaders are continuing to call for a restorative understanding of policing and incarceration. In *Beyond Prisons: A New Interfaith Paradigm for Our Failed Prison System*, Laura Magnani and Harmon L. Wray offer a thought-provoking analysis of the present policing and corrections systems. By adopting a "restorative justice" approach, they argue, the public experiences not only a reduction in crime and violence, but also a savings of millions of dollars that could be used for education and/or economic development for all. Magnani and Wray, in reflecting on the present system, observe: "Present prison policy demonstrates that we do not believe that prisoners can repent, show remorse, and work toward healing themselves and their relationships. When the weakest or most impoverished among us does not experience the support or sustaining balance of a healthy society, we are not a just society. Just as when survivors of serious crime are unheard, marginalized, or exploited, when offenders suffer the unending isolation of our prisons [and jails] we can hardly lay claim to justice."[13]

Both activists and criminal justice officials alike are calling for a reclaiming of the restorative justice/rehabilitation model, especially for non-violent offenders. This model recognizes the complexity of issues regarding the factors and influences contributing to arrests, incarceration, recidivism, etc. By approaching the corrections/jailing process from the restorative justice perspective, we are empowered to further ensure public safety while also reducing the financial burden to taxpayers, and also contributing to the restoration of families and communities. The following proposals build on the Alternative to Incarceration (ATI) Program of the Division of Probation and Correctional Alternatives in the New York State Counties and the City of New York.[14]

Overall, we must call for collaboration and a prophetic, passionate, determined, and persistent coalition to inject a sense of humanity back into the social, political, and economic systems of American society by calling for and working together, hand in hand, heart to heart, to:

1. Establish a living wage for all Americans, extending unemployment benefits effectively and indefinitely, ensuring that every family has a viable path toward the dignity of labor and the honor of providing for itself and its community.

2. Eradicate "mass incarceration"; reform related human rights atrocities; end the privatization of prisons in the state of Georgia and nationally; repeal the "Stand Your Ground" laws; encourage alternative sentencing, including programs for reentry, prevention, and drug treatment.

3. Reform national immigration policies with a viable and humane path-to-citizenship policy, affirming the DREAM Act for Latino students; increase social programs for immigrant families, regardless of status.

13. Laura Magnani and Harmon L. Wray, *Beyond Prisons: A New Interfaith Paradigm for Our Failed Prison System* (Minneapolis: Augsburg Fortress, 2006), 14-15.
14. http://dpca.state.ny.us/ati_description.htm.

4. Rebuild America's schools, creating funding equality from city to city and region to region, empowering local communities to share educational outcomes in partnership with national and state governing bodies; paying students a national standard of quality wages and benefits; providing holistic support for student families and services that encourage education, creativity, and innovation at all levels; student loan debt forgiveness for low-income students; and investing in higher education for all Americans.

Conclusion

Mahatma Gandhi declared, "We must become the change that we seek." Now is the time, now is our time, to restore justice and human dignity to our systems, to affirm the inherent value and worth of all God's children, ensuring that future generations will see that we are a people who are fully human and celebrate the spirit of God moving and circulating through the veins of creation, in our time and the time to come!

Now is the time, now is our time, to restore justice, humanity, and equality to the very foundation of our democracy, and to fight like hell for what is right, what is true, and what is just in the world. The passage, Revelation 21:1-4, proclaiming God's vision of a new heaven and a new earth is a fitting image of what it means to build the world house for our time and engage in the ongoing task of prophetic protest in its multiple dimensions.

Here the writer of Revelation places the creation of God's new world in dramatic terms:

> Then I saw a new heaven and a new earth, for the first heaven and the first earth had passed away, and there was no longer any sea. I saw the Holy City, the new Jerusalem, coming down out of heaven from God, prepared as a bride beautifully dressed for her husband. And I heard a loud voice from the throne saying, "Now the dwelling of God is with men, and he will live with them. They will be his people, and God himself will be with them and be their God. He will wipe every tear from their eyes. There will be no more death or mourning or crying or pain, for the old order of things has passed away." (NIV)

Make no mistake; indeed, these are difficult days in which we now live. In the words of Thomas Paine on the eve of signing the Declaration of

Independence, truly "these are the times that try men's souls." Yet, there is something powerful happening in our world today. It is as if a new world is coming into being, a world of difference and plurality, where the bonds of slavery and bondage are breaking and old limitations are changing into new possibilities. In January 2013 the world was watching as the first black president of the United States of America, President Barack Hussein Obama, took the oath of office for a second historic term. To win in 2008 was a miraculous feat in itself, but to win again in 2012 was not only miraculous but may even have been divine. The historic nature of Obama's second inauguration in Washington, D.C., does not make sense apart from the long struggle for freedom and human dignity, apart from the sorrows of our enslaved African ancestors who stepped upon these shores more than four hundred years ago in chains, to those who endured over a hundred years of racialized Jim Crow segregation, and yes even now to millions living in the shadows of history's pain, as the legacy of slavery and Jim Crow can be felt in the cries of millions of impoverished and over a million and a half blacks in jails and prisons across the nation.

Despite all the challenges that we see in our world today, the writer of Revelation reminds us that God breaks into human history to establish a new world — to make of this old world a new world — a world of peace, justice, human dignity, and freedom for all God's children and the flourishing of creation in all its dimensions. The irony of President Obama's inauguration is that it occurred on the same day on which we commemorate one of the greatest Americans this country has ever known, Dr. Martin Luther King Jr. The year 2013 marks the 50th anniversary of the March on Washington and the historic "I Have a Dream" speech. It also marks the 150th anniversary of the signing of the Emancipation Proclamation. Both events set in motion unfolding dramas of freedom and justice, a drumbeat of human dignity marching through history like a mighty army. The year Dr. King delivered the "I Have a Dream" speech, on August 28, 1963, the struggles of the civil rights movement were at their fiercest.

Coming just off the heels of the Freedom Rides of 1961 when students from across the North and Northeast boarded buses and rode across the South protesting, challenging, and dismantling the laws of segregation, with leaders now turning their attention from segregated lunch counters to voting rights, Dr. King and his leaders descended on Birmingham, Alabama (what some called Bombingham). It was there that King wrote the famed "Letter from Birmingham Jail" on strips of tissue paper, in which he proclaimed that "injustice anywhere is a threat to justice everywhere" and that it is the responsibility of all of us to stand up for justice, freedom, and equality wherever we see injustice in the world. That same passionate determination led Dr. King to speak out against the war in Vietnam and then to introduce the Poor People's Campaign where he would organize the poor people of the nation to establish a "bill of rights for the poor" as an amendment to the Constitution of the United States of America.

On the day prior to April 4, 1968, the day he was assassinated, he was scheduled to preach at his home church, Ebenezer Baptist Church in Atlanta. But there were striking sanitation workers in Memphis who called for him. They were planning a march. The mood was tense and the atmosphere violent. King's friends in the movement warned him against attending. But because of his commitment to the cause, he went. Although he was tired, he went out to the Masonic Temple and delivered what we now know as the great "Mountaintop" speech. In the speech, he concluded, "But it really doesn't matter with me now, because I've been to the mountaintop." "Like anybody (he said), I would like to live a long life, longevity has its place . . . but I'm not concerned about that now and he's allowed me to look over and I've seen the Promised Land." Even as his countenance changed, with a glare of powerful determination and resolution, he said, "I may not get there with you, but we as a people will get to the Promised Land." "I'm not fearing any man, mine eyes have seen the glory of the coming of the Lord."

Now, as we reflect fifty years later on his dream, his life, and his legacy, it is as if we can see the dream of Dr. King unfolding. That bursting into being is the kingdom of God, the making of a new heaven and a new earth, and though it has yet to be fully realized, it seems as though we see glimpses of the power and brilliance of God's new world being made possible.

I resonate with that on a personal level. As I have said, I was raised in the belly of the South. We were poor but loved. Like the men in Memphis, my father was a sanitation worker. So in a real sense, Dr. King was marching for men like my father and others at the margins of society, who did the hard work of removing the waste from homes and ensuring clean neighborhoods and communities. He did the work no one else wanted to do, the bottom of the barrel duty work of society. There were days that I would join with him as he worked and would see the filth and grime of raw sewage circulating at the plants and experience the smell that was too horrid to bear, yet he and his fellows would engage in this work with dignity and grace.

What I find so compelling about the legacy of Dr. King is that he stood with the least of these and the lowliest of these, those who (as

Howard Thurman says) stand with their "backs against the wall," who struggle every day with the threat of nihilism and homelessness and despair. Because he stood up for men like my father, I have dedicated my life to the same struggle for freedom, justice, and equality. We all should have some cause or some struggle that we are willing to stand up and fight for. Now, more than ever before, with the rise of drug activity in our communities, where drug selling and incarceration have become the normative pattern of life, where sisters are forced to sell their bodies to feed their children, where it's harder to go to college than to go to jail — it's time to stand up and reclaim the legacy of standing and sitting, singing and marching, shouting and crying, to make this world a better place for our time and for generations to come.

Reclaiming the Dream

Reclaiming the dream of Dr. King today and building the world house mean doing our part to help make and remake America into what it can be. While we honor the reelection of President Obama for another four years, the fact is that neither he nor any elected official can bring about change alone. It's up to each of us now more than ever before to stand up and fight, speak out, march, protest, sing, vote, give, hope, love, read, laugh, cry, and do whatever is necessary so that we might become the change that we seek. Once I was driving from Missouri to Kentucky and I had car problems crossing the bridge into Paducah, Kentucky. It was very late at night. It was a two-lane bridge, so there was no way to pull over to the side. I started downshifting to get my car to go a little farther, but it continued to slow down. I made it to an off-ramp on the other side of the bridge, and then the car finally shut off. I was still blocking the road and, with railings on both sides, there was no place to go. I got out of the car, and with the steering wheel in my right hand and the door in my left, I started pushing the car. It was an old 1984 Mercury Capri, and it weighed a ton. Just as my legs were about to give out, some men from the store across the road and another man who had been driving by ran to my aid and helped me push the car to a safe spot. Over the next four years, like never before in our lives, we have got to help push this car we call a democracy to where it should be. We've got to do our part.

Secondly, we've got to work together. Rich and poor, black and white, Christian, Muslim, and Hindu, we must move swiftly toward King's vision of the beloved community that taught us that all life is interrelated. The rise of technology and consumerism has led to isolation and rugged individuality, to the extent that there is a deep and profound distrust that we have toward each other, especially in the black experience. We have become victims of our own success. But God is calling us to help make way for the new heaven and new earth coming into being, a world where we learn to "treat everybody right," and where they sing, "walk together children, don't you get weary, there's a great camp meeting in the promised land!"

Finally, reclaiming the dream of Dr. King, building the world house, in our present age, and certainly making way for the reign of God and the coming of God's new heaven and new earth, mean to keep hoping, keep living, keep loving, keep working, keep forgiving, keep studying, keep imagining, keep walking, keep talking, keep wishing, and keep dreaming for a better day. The weight of poverty and violence has seemed to quench the flaming passions of justice, liberation, and resilience in the face of so much pain and suffering today. But I believe that God is raising a new generation of men and women unafraid to tell the truth, to speak truth to power, to fight for what's right, and to make real the dream of Dr. King.

Then we can sing aloud with James Weldon Johnson:

> Lift every voice and sing,
> till earth and heaven ring,
> ring with the harmonies of liberty;
> let our rejoicing rise
> high as the listening skies,
> let it resound loud as the rolling sea.
> . . . God of our weary years,
> God of our silent tears,
> thou who hast brought us thus far on the way;
> thou who hast by thy might led us into the light,
> keep us forever in the path, we pray.
> Lest our feet stray from the places, our God, where we met thee;
> lest our hearts drunk with the wine of the world, we forget thee,
> shadowed beneath thy hand,
> may we forever stand,
> true to our God,
> true to our native land.

Bibliography

Aptheker, Herbert. *David Walker's Appeal: Its Setting and Its Meaning.* New York: Humanities Press, 1965.

Asante, Molefi Kete. *Afrocentricity.* Trenton, N.J.: African World Press, 1988.

———. *The Afrocentric Idea.* Philadelphia: Temple University Press, 1998.

Balia, Daryl M. *Christian Resistance to Apartheid.* Johannesburg: Skotaville Publishers, 1989.

Battle, Michael. *Reconciliation: The Ubuntu Theology of Desmond Tutu.* Cleveland: Pilgrim Press, 1997.

Beardsworth, Richard. *Derrida and the Political.* New York: Routledge, 1996.

Bennett, Lerone, Jr. *What Manner of Man: A Memorial Biography of Martin Luther King, Jr.* New York: Pocket Books, 1968.

Borer, Tristan Anne. *Challenging the State: Churches as Political Actors in South Africa, 1980-1994.* Notre Dame, Ind.: University of Notre Dame Press, 1998.

Branch, Taylor. *Parting the Waters: America in the King Years, 1954-63.* New York: Simon and Schuster, 1988.

Browning, Gary K. *Lyotard and the End of Grand Narratives.* Cardiff, U.K.: University of Wales Press, 2000.

Cobb, John B. *Postmodernism and Public Policy: Reframing Religion, Culture, Education, Sexuality, Class, Race, Politics, and the Economy.* Albany: State University of New York Press, 2002.

Cone, James H. "The Theology of Martin Luther King, Jr." *Union Seminary Quarterly Review* 40, no. 4 (1986): 24.

———. *Martin and Malcolm and America: A Dream or a Nightmare.* Maryknoll, N.Y.: Orbis, 2000.

———. *The Cross and the Lynching Tree.* Maryknoll, N.Y.: Orbis, 2011.

Bibliography

Critchley, Simon. *The Ethics of Deconstruction: Derrida and Levinas.* Cambridge: Blackwell, 1992.

Curry, George E., ed. *The Affirmative Action Debate.* Cambridge, Mass.: Perseus Books, 1996.

Deane, Herbert. *The Political and Social Ideas of St. Augustine.* New York: Columbia University Press, 1963.

Dear, John. *The God of Peace: Toward a Theology of Nonviolence.* Maryknoll, N.Y.: Orbis, 1994.

De Gruchy, John W., and Charles Villa-Vicencio. *Apartheid Is a Heresy.* Grand Rapids: Eerdmans, 1983.

Derrida, Jacques. *Writing and Difference.* Translated by Alan Bass. London: Routledge and Kegan Paul, 1978.

—————. "A Word of Welcome." In *Adieu to Emmanuel Levinas,* translated by Pascale-Anne Brault and Michael Nass, 15-123, 135-52. Stanford: Stanford University Press, 1999.

DeWolf, Harold L. *A Theology of the Living Church.* Rev. ed. New York: Harper and Row, 1960; original 1953.

—————. *Crime and Justice in America: A Paradox of Conscience.* New York: Harper and Row, 1975.

Eisenstadt, Oona. "The Problem of the Promise: Derrida on Levinas on the Cities of Refuge." *Cross Currents* 52, no. 4 (Winter 2003): 474-82.

Elshtain, Jean Bethke. *Public Man, Private Woman: Women in Social and Political Thought.* Princeton: Princeton University Press, 1981.

—————. *Augustine and the Limits of Politics.* Notre Dame, Ind.: University of Notre Dame Press, 1995.

Ferreira, M. Jamie. "'Total Altruism' in Levinas's 'Ethics of the Welcome.'" *Journal of Religious Ethics* 29, no. 3 (2001): 443-70.

Frost, Brian. *Struggling to Forgive: Nelson Mandela and South Africa's Search for Reconciliation.* London: HarperCollins, 1998.

Garrow, David J. *Bearing the Cross: Martin Luther King, Jr., and the Southern Christian Leadership Conference.* New York: Vintage Books, 1988.

Gibbs, Robert, "Emmanual Levinas (1906-1995): Introduction." In *The Postmodern God: A Theological Reader,* edited by Graham Ward. Malden, Mass.: Blackwell, 1997.

Hill, Johnny Bernard. *The Theology of Martin Luther King Jr. and Desmond Mpilo Tutu.* New York: Palgrave Macmillan, 2007.

—————. *The First Black President: Barack Obama, Race, Politics, and the American Dream.* New York: Palgrave Macmillan, 2009.

Howells, Christina. *Derrida: Deconstruction from Phenomenology to Ethics.* Malden, Mass.: Blackwell Publishers and Polity Press, 1999.

Kelley, Robin D. G. *Freedom Dreams: The Black Radical Imagination.* Boston: Beacon Press, 2002.

King, Martin Luther, Jr. *Stride toward Freedom: The Montgomery Story.* New York: Harper and Row, 1958.

————. *Strength to Love.* Philadelphia: Fortress, 1963.

————. *Why We Can't Wait.* New York: Harper and Row, 1963.

————. *Where Do We Go from Here: Chaos or Community?* New York: Harper and Row, 1967.

————. *The Autobiography of Martin Luther King, Jr.* Edited by Clayborne Carson. New York: Warner Books, 1998.

Kretzschmar, Louise. *The Voice of Black Theology in South Africa.* Johannesburg: Raven Press, 1983.

Levinas, Emmanuel. *Of God Who Comes to Mind.* Translated by Bettina Bergo. Stanford: Stanford University Press, 1986.

Lincoln, C. Eric, and Lawrence H. Mamiya. *The Black Church in the African American Experience.* Durham, N.C.: Duke University Press, 1990.

Long, D. Stephen. *Divine Economy: Theology and the Market.* New York: Routledge, 2000.

Lyotard, Jean-François. *The Postmodern Condition: A Report on Knowledge.* Translated by Geoff Bennington and Brian Massumi. Minneapolis: University of Minnesota Press, 1984.

————. *The Differend: Phases in Dispute.* Translated by G. Van Den Abbeele. Manchester: Manchester University Press, 1988.

Malcolm X. *The Autobiography of Malcolm X, with Alex Haley.* New York: Ballantine Books, 1973.

Marx, Karl, and Friedrich Engels. *The Communist Manifesto.* New York: International Publishers, 1932.

Melendez, Guillermo. *Seeds of Promise: The Prophetic Church in Central America.* New York: Friendship Press, 1990.

Milbank, John. *The Word Made Strange: Theology, Language, Culture.* Malden, Mass.: Blackwell, 1997.

Milbank, John, Catherine Pickstock, and Graham Ward, eds. *Radical Orthodoxy: A New Theology.* London and New York: Routledge, 1999.

Moltmann, Jürgen. *Theology of Hope.* New York: Harper and Row, 1967.

————. *The Way of Jesus Christ: Christologies in Messianic Dimensions.* Minneapolis: Fortress, 1993.

Moynihan, Daniel. *The Negro Family: A Case for National Action.* Washington, D.C.: U.S. Government Printing Office, 1965.

Niebuhr, Reinhold. *Nature and Destiny of Man.* Englewood Cliffs, N.J.: Prentice-Hall, 1964.

————. *Moral Man and Immoral Society: A Study in Ethics and Politics.* Louisville: Westminster John Knox, 2001.

Novak, Michael. *Will It Liberate? Questions about Liberation Theology.* New York: Paulist, 1986.

————. *The Catholic Ethic and the Spirit of Capitalism*. New York: Free Press, 1993.

O'Donovan, Oliver. *The Desire of the Nations: Rediscovering the Roots of Political Theology*. Cambridge: Cambridge University Press, 1996.

————. *Resurrection and Moral Order: An Outline for Evangelical Ethics*. Grand Rapids: Eerdmans, 2001.

Raines, Howard. *My Soul Is Rested: The Story of the Civil Rights Movement in the Deep South*. New York: Penguin Books, 1983.

Roberts, J. Deotis. *Liberation and Reconciliation*. Maryknoll, N.Y.: Orbis, 1994.

Robinson, Cedric J. *Black Marxism: The Making of the Black Radical Tradition*. Chapel Hill: University of North Carolina Press, 1983.

Tutu, Desmond. *The Rainbow People of God: The Making of a Peaceful Revolution*. Edited by John Allen. New York: Doubleday, 1994.

————. *No Future without Forgiveness*. New York: Doubleday, 1997.

Ward, Graham. *Theology and Contemporary Critical Theory*. New York: St. Martin's Press, 1996.

West, Cornel. *Prophesy Deliverance! An Afro-American Revolutionary Christianity*. Philadelphia: Westminster, 1982.

————. *Beyond Eurocentrism and Multiculturalism*. Vol. 1, *Prophetic Thought in Postmodern Times*. Monroe, Maine: Common Courage Press, 1993.

————. *Race Matters*. Boston: Beacon Press, 1993.

————. *The Cornel West Reader*. New York: Basic Civitas Books, 1999.

Williams, James. "The Last Refuge from Nihilism." *International Journal of Philosophical Studies* 8, no. 1 (2000): 115-24.

————. *Lyotard and the Political*. New York: Routledge, 2000.

Wilmore, Gayraud S. *Black Religion and Black Radicalism: An Interpretation of the Religious History of African Americans*. 3rd ed. Maryknoll, N.Y.: Orbis, 1998.

Wiltse, Charles M., ed. *David Walker's Appeal*. New York: Hill and Wang, 1965.

Wright, Richard. *Black Power: A Record of Reactions in a Land of Pathos*. New York: Harper and Brothers, 1954.

Young, Henry J. *Major Black Religious Leaders, 1755-1940*. Nashville: Abingdon, 1977.

Žižek, Slavoj. *The Fragile Absolute; or, Why Is the Christian Legacy Worth Fighting For?* London: Verso, 2000.

Index

Index

CPSIA information can be obtained
at www.ICGtesting.com
Printed in the USA
FSHW011803051121
85959FS